T0072297

TAP INTO THE
POWER OF GOD
A GUIDE TO SPIRITUAL GROWTH

DANIELLE C. PACE

BALBOA.PRESS

A DIVISION OF HAY HOUSE

Balboa Press books may be ordered through booksellers or by contacting:

Balboa Press
A Division of Hay House
1663 Liberty Drive
Bloomington, IN 47403
www.balboapress.com
844-682-1282

Because of the dynamic nature of the Internet, any web addresses or
links contained in this book may have changed since publication and
may no longer be valid. The views expressed in this work are solely those
of the author and do not necessarily reflect the views of the publisher,
and the publisher hereby disclaims any responsibility for them.

The author of this book does not dispense medical advice or prescribe the use
of any technique as a form of treatment for physical, emotional, or medical
problems without the advice of a physician, either directly or indirectly. The
intent of the author is only to offer information of a general nature to help
you in your quest for emotional and spiritual well-being. In the event you use
any of the information in this book for yourself, which is your constitutional
right, the author and the publisher assume no responsibility for your actions.

Any people depicted in stock imagery provided by Getty Images are
models, and such images are being used for illustrative purposes only.
Certain stock imagery © Getty Images.

Cover Art by John Bell at SelfPubBookCovers.com/JohnBellArt

Print information available on the last page.

ISBN: 979-8-7652-2756-5 (sc)
ISBN: 979-8-7652-2757-2 (e)

Balboa Press rev. date: 06/07/2022

Dedicated to God
Whose love moves all mountains,
even those we build around our hearts

Contents

Introduction

Self-aware thoughts separate man from all other life on this planet, but what we choose to think can separate us from God, our true self and each other. Thoughts can create or thoughts can destroy. The purpose of this book is to help you tap into divine thought and turn your thoughts to better serve you. If, as researchers are now finding, our thoughts are creating form, then we are responsible for what we choose to think, to see and what we choose to become.

A change in perspective can lead to a change in your thoughts and that is why I am writing this book. I went through such a change that was quite miraculous. The change wasn't instantaneous. It took place over a couple of years. It all began at the very lowest point of my life, when I was contemplating suicide. Some people would say suicide is a sin, but I think if you asked God, God would say He loves all His creations and wants us to think again. I was lucky enough to find a 12 step program that introduced me to the loving God that would not condemn me, or anyone else, to an eternity of pain for being sad or for any other reason. During the course of taking these 12 steps, I learned to identify my truth and tap into the divine source of wisdom which is God who is now both a part of me and all around me. I decided not to waste any more of my time here thinking unworthy thoughts. God gave us our brains and choice so that we would use these to seek the Truth. God revealed to me that we are all divine as we are part of Him and He lives in us all. We are all miracles. We are made in God's image. Scientists estimate the odds of any one of us being born on this planet as life capable of self-awareness is one in 400 trillion! So basically there is zero chance of you being here as you are, divine, so how can your existence not be a miracle?

Why aren't we taught in school about the miracle that we are? About our uniqueness and our special talents and our ability to communicate with our Creator from a very young age? Why are we pigeon-holed by education with laborious tests and told what we can and cannot do? The truth is you can do whatever you think you can do, so think again! Write down your thoughts. Dream big dreams. If we all did this, where would WE collectively be? Go back to when you were a kid with a wild imagination. What things did you want to accomplish that were truly important? Re-imagine how you will make an impact and start again with just one step. Why lose any of that zest for life you once possessed?

I am writing this book because I gained back my joy and my faith in God and my fellow man and my vivid imagination. I know now that anything is possible. I know I am loved by God and that I am an important messenger of His ever-advancing creation. I want to share my experience because others here may be suffering because of their thoughts, as I was. The answer is God wants us to think again. God wants you to be happy, joyous and free. We do not have to live our lives separate from God, our true selves, and each other. God wants us to know and love Him, love ourselves, and love others as ourselves. It makes sense that we should do this if you think about it. Everyone benefits when any one among us sees the light. What if we all saw the light? What miracles could we create to heal ourselves and our beloved planet?

In this text, I have re-imagined the 12 step solution that helped me tap into divine thought as a generic process to help the reader connect to the Great Spirit of the Universe. The aim is to tap into this strength daily. This is not a new religion and doesn't aim to replace your religion. It is a spiritual approach to finding your truth. A design for a life of freedom from fear, anger and depression that only God can provide. As far as gender goes, I do not think that God is a male or a female, but a combination of the best masculine and feminine traits available. For the purposes of writing this book only, I am referring to the Master of the Universe, as God or He. In my eyes, He or She is strong, reliable, steadfast, loving, kind and accepting. Feel free to substitute any other name or pronoun for what I have chosen as you desire. Your

"God" is personal to you and your relationship should be what you make of it. This book does not attempt to tell you what to believe, but attempts to help you get in touch with a spiritual power that has colossal abilities to be of service to you if sought.

Here are the 12 steps, as I have re-imagined them, to help anyone establish a connection to the divine:

1. Are You Done Yet?
2. Are You Willing to Believe?
3. If So, Get on Your Knees
4. Examine Your Past Fearlessly
5. Admit The Truth
6. Identify Your Deficiencies
7. Ask God to Remove Them
8. Make a List of Those You Have Wronged
9. Make Amends
10. Continue to Review Daily
11. Seek God Thru Prayer & Meditation
12. Carry the Message to Others

Chasing or Being Pursued?

"For as this appalling ocean surrounds the verdant land, so in the soul of man there lies one insular Tahiti, full of peace and joy, but encompassed by all the horrors of the half-known life. God keep thee! Push not off from that isle, thou canst never return!"- Herman Melville "Moby Dick", CHAPTER 58, The Brit. Paragraph 12

As Ahab faced the great whale, I'd like to think the sea held it's breath in rapt suspense at the encroachment of man and the battle to be waged for it's own eminence. As it railed at man's audacity, did it cheer for the great Moby Dick? We all must face down our demons whether those of our own making, or those provided by outside sources strictly to confound and confuse us. Those elusive answers, why am I here, what is it all for, I had been chasing in my thoughts and not finding any good answers. The chase almost destroyed me as Ahab's relentless pursuit of the great white whale destroyed him. But suddenly the keeper of all those secrets, that great entity, my own Creator, turned around to confront me, to question my compulsion for answers. He turned the tables to show me what I sought with my thoughts, barraging me from all sides and it was equal parts terrifying and exhilarating. Terrifying because I couldn't be sure this was not some demon come to torment me. Exhilarating when I was sure it was my savior come to rescue me. And I was tossed about like Ahab's ship, The Pequod, without shelter, in an open sea, rudderless. The storm had come.

God came to show me He was the rudder, and the keeper of all the knowledge that could calm the mighty sea. When He turned to face me, I knew I had been naive to pursue what I could never comprehend. I tried to turn from this entity, back to the unasking, the unknowing back to making my way unaware of His persistent presence and His dominion. But as Melville said so rightly, I had pushed off from that isle. It was too late to turn back. But now, I was no longer chasing, I was being pursued.

I had been living my own version of the half-known life, when this began, I was depressed, angry, addicted to alcohol and I wanted to leave this confounding world and be at peace. I knew there had to be something more meaningful than this depressing life. Soon clues to the puzzle began appearing everywhere. As I started unlocking and deciphering them, my life, my "one insular Tahiti", slowly became filled with trials and tribulations not unlike a great storm on the ocean. I was traveling into that storm and found I couldn't turn back. The ocean was roiling around me and fear overcame me. In hindsight, I believe this was The Great Universal Spirit drawing me in to confront me. It was within this storm, and seeing no way out, that I cursed God, certain that he was against me, as my ego kept assuring me. My ego would not admit defeat and surrender to God. It couldn't. And so, the battle began. The war between my ego and my God. This is a book about that struggle and the resolution which led to my ultimate surrender and placing myself under God's management.

Somehow facing this storm changed me spiritually. I can see now that all of the tribulations I faced during my life were because I was meant for something more. That the life I was living was not a life to be proud of, and not the one God wanted for me. I can't explain the storm that confronted me or how I had somehow, in my suicidal blundering and constant pursuit of meaning, wandered into it. It seems I had an overabundance of faith in my own abilities and I had lost faith in anything but my own ego and so the storm came to test me. I was certain that I could figure a way out of it on my own. Circumstances began to seem far from circumstantial, as I seemed to be chased farther into the storms depths, more delusional and more depressed. I was confronted with the duality of this world. The good and the bad of it. The ambiguity of choices, thoughts and unintended results. Even though I meant well, my decisions back-fired. Each decision I made in seeming good faith producing unforeseen consequences. I felt I was being chased into some invisible snare that changed shape to encompass me after every seemingly cautious decision I made. When I finally lost all faith in my own abilities to escape impending disaster, my ego convinced me, the only escape was to end my life. I know it was not, and could never have been, a logical choice. Even in hindsight I wonder how I could have been so misled.

I know now that my ego was trapped into choosing between suicide and surrender. The ego would never choose to surrender to God. This would mean the ego had lost control. Ironically, all of it's spite for God came out as it realized there was no other way out. I believe it was my curses shouted to God at this bitter end that somehow turned the tide. The very fact that I reached out to blame God, so certain of His existence yet sure of His apathy, was, I believe, the turning point. Looking back I can see just how perilous my predicament really was. I was too proud to ask God for help and my ego was cornered and fighting to keep me drinking and in the dark. My ego tried to convince me there was nothing out there for me to find. Life had no meaning and very shortly would be over. But God had other plans. Now He was turning on the light.

When God began pursuing me and revelations first started coming, I was sure I was going insane. Someone or something was challenging me with my own reflection. Some entity knew things about me that no one but me could possibly know. It was confronting me about things I did or did not do. It was like someone was watching me through my own eyes. I was afraid to look in the mirror, so I covered all the mirrors with sheets, but it didn't stop. Funny how my ego told me suicide was not insane but an all-knowing presence taunting me from the great beyond was! In hindsight, I realize it was my higher power, the all-knowing God that came to challenge my ego for His place. He came to test my fears, show me that no defense I made against them would ever be enough to keep them at bay. God wanted me to know I had a choice. I could choose faith in the good or let fear convince me of the bad. I could take a leap of faith and trust God, or insist on going it alone. I had to choose. I could live my life through faith or destroy my life through fear.

This was why God had pursued me. Had I really ever given God His will in my life? Hadn't my ego always taken precedence? I couldn't deny it. Had I ever relied on God and not myself? No, I prided myself on how self-reliant I was! I also had no idea the tricks my ego employed to keep me from knowing the sheer futility of self-reliance at the time. I didn't understand that these wiles were the reason I could not be happy, joyous or free. Whenever I got to a level in life that I thought would bring joy, I had a new hunger for something else. Why was I never allowed the peace and joy I sought for very long. I was playing whack-a-mole at life quite unaware the joke was on me until the whole board popped up and all my best shots no longer hit their mark. My ego turned me towards alcohol, a temporary fix for my fears and a temporary relief. But this led to more depression which increased my fears. All I had left, in the end, was desperation, fear and utter hopelessness.

This is how my journey began. A life of no purpose, insane thoughts, and a crazy captain at the helm of my ship, bent on self-destruction. This is when God came to pursue me. To find out if I really wanted a life full of fear or if I intended to surrender to a life that was happy, joyous and free. Are you being pursued by God? Have you left your island of self-reliance, in a search for greater meaning than the half-known life, only to find God hot on your trail? If so, this book asks you to open your mind to faith and a belief in the unknown. Your ego will not allow this easily. You have been taught to rely on yourself all of your life. The ego is in charge here and it reinforces your belief in it everyday through fear and choice-less choices. By changing management and hiring God, who knows all, as your new Commander, you are essentially firing your ego, your Captain Ahab. He will not leave his cushy captains' seat without a fight. Also, you will have to learn his tricks so he cannot return to destroy you and your new-found freedom.

A New Design

Drinking had slowly crept up on me, but being suicidal happened suddenly and really scared me. The thought that it seemed to make sense was even more terrifying. What I finally decided was that it was that age old spirit, alcohol, that was driving me to feel this way. I even thought I was becoming schizophrenic from the effects it had on me, so I decided to stop drinking. I was scared if I told anyone my thoughts, they would lock me in an institution, so I suffered my suicidal thoughts and delusions in silence. I made many failed attempts then to quit drinking. A friend would invite me out for dinner and I would end up having "just one glass" or I'd buy alcohol "for company" and end up drinking it myself. A particularly stressful day always seemed to be the norm and a good reason to need a drink. I stopped buying alcohol, but it kept finding me. I moved to put distance between my old drinking spots and myself many times, but that didn't work either. Nothing was working. I found that I couldn't quit on my own.

They say in *Alcoholics Anonymous (AA)* the disease of alcoholism is "cunning, baffling and powerful." I think all addictions are this way. They trap you into believing the fear that you cannot get through your day without them. God can help you if you ask him in your morning devotion for a reprieve from this fear and from the addiction for just this day. He will grant you this reprieve every day you ask for it. That is why we say "One day at a time" in AA.

I kept trying to quit drinking on my own for about 6 months and I did manage to cut down a little but never to stop! What was going on? My Mama Lucy had always talked about AA and how it helped her to quit drinking. Having alcohol to blame for my seemingly insane thoughts was a huge relief. I thought I could go to AA and get fixed, and then maybe I wouldn't want to die anymore. No more boogeyman in the mirror either. So I went to my first AA meeting. It was really hard to stay sober, but I managed to white-knuckle it because I was finally meeting people and making friends that didn't drink. I got support from them to stay away from my old habits. But it wasn't easy because I didn't want to get a sponsor. I didn't want to admit I was an alcoholic and I didn't want to do the steps that everyone said would keep me sober and give me a life I could only dream of. Also they said I had to let a higher power help me. Even though I wasn't drinking, I was still having insane thoughts. Why did I have to rely on a higher power? I had been told by a

Pastor that God would send me to hell if I got a divorce, but because, at the time I valued my life, I had gotten one anyways. Was this who would help me? The very God I had cursed? The One who was now following and taunting me?

But it seems God wanted me to move forward, and I wasn't going to escape Him. I had to admit I needed His help if I was going to try this 12 step cure, and I was desperate to try it. At the time I didn't realize that my ego was throwing up roadblocks trying to convince me to backslide. Hurricane Irma caused many missed meetings and I started being tempted to drink. My son was in a bad accident and I slipped. I was so emotional about everything that had happened and too busy feeling sorry for myself to go out with my new-found sober friends, but luckily they didn't give up on me. In AA, there is a saying that the fellowship will love you until you love yourself. I went to a beach meeting in Madeira Beach and afterward, while I was lying on the beach, a girl from the meeting came up to me. I remembered her because she was tiny but shared how she is in the tree service industry and takes chain saws and climbs up into trees for a living! She was walking down the beach in her Redwing boots! You really can't make this stuff up. She introduced herself and said that the beach meeting wasn't a real meeting and I should come with her to the one she was chairing. So I started going to her meetings and in the process made a great sober friend.

Of course my ego was still fighting for it's own survival. The belief in a power greater than myself would doom it to oblivion. Even though I believed God to be there, I was still way too wrapped up in my ego and thought I could do this alone. I went to the meetings, but they did not fix me. I read all the AA literature, but I didn't really understand how it applied to me. All of my best efforts didn't fix me, once again. What finally helped was getting an AA sponsor, trusting her and doing the work prescribed in the 12 steps of the *Big Book of Alcoholics Anonymous*. Somewhere in that process, I started understanding the war that was waging and that I wasn't insane at all. God wanted my attention!

During the process of doing the steps, I was able to see the role my ego had played throughout my life and how it had almost destroyed me with it's hundred forms of fear and backwards priorities. God had been shadowing it and in essence me, waiting for me to realize He alone had the answers. The ones He wanted me to know would slowly be revealed through my faith. They were not all for me to know, though. I had to admit maybe I did not need to know all the answers. All I had to do was accept that He knew. Have faith in His plan. And He knew me. He had seen me and my search and had been there all along waiting for me to recognize His presence. It was nothing for Him to show me, to confront me. I had opened the door and He had walked through it. I could no longer deny God's existence. He wanted me to acknowledge His number one spot. That I **was** and **always will be** a piece of Him and that **I am** only **because of Him**. The insanity I felt was Him fighting my ego to give me that knowledge. I had to be willing to acknowledge His presence inside me and change my perception or my ego would convince me life was futile and that I should end it all.

God showed me the result of my own best advice. He let me know I was at the crossroads of a certain self-led path towards hopelessness and to a bitter end, or a faith-led step into an unknown, unmarked path. Only He could know where the path led. It would require faith for me to tread that path. I ventured into that great unknown. In hindsight, I realize that the second step of AA was my first leap of faith in a series of leaps leading to my total belief in a benevolent and supreme power guiding all mankind forward in this universe.

I never knew the 12 steps of AA were actually a new design for living until I was half-way through taking them. By taking them, I was slowly replacing a purposeless self-led, self-centered way of life with one where I was given a purpose that would actually fulfill my ambitions and bring forth the peace and joy I had always sought. I had to be released from the insanity that I could know and control everything and everyone and finally admit that self-reliance would always fail me. I had to step out in faith. I had asked to know and I was shown the truth. The truth was I would never know what He knows! But I don't need to because He does. When I let my new manager (my higher power, God) take over and show me where I had been wrong, and allow Him to change my perspective, I was slowly released from the chains I had put on myself by listening to my ego. My hubris turned to a new found innocence. I could go back to being a child and having a protector. I could have faith and be happy day by day. I wasn't required to know everything. The greatest part of Him is now available to me. As my Manager He is always available for a consult night and day! No appointment necessary. I do not need to know the why and how of everything. I have access to the Source of Everything.

Do You Need a New Manager?

If you feel like something is lacking in your finances, health or relationships, you are not alone. The self-help book industry is thriving despite how many of these books have already sold. If self-help really worked, someone would put all the answers in one book, get rich and nobody would have any problems. It seems that we all have issues managing our time, health, money and relationships. Is the answer reading another self-help book? I think maybe it is time to admit that the self-reliance principles that we have been taught henceforth are failing us. With the hectic pace of life and the need for two income families, stress-filled days are now the norm. What if you allowed a new manager to step in and run your life? One with all the answers? One who is in your corner and always around to give you advice and help you push through any problems you encounter day to day. One who can point you in the right direction in all your dilemmas.

There is much conflicting information out there as warring factions compete for your attention. It is easy to be led astray by schemes to help you get rich quick, lose weight, get the relationship you deserve. Would these things really fulfill your life? What if you discovered a manager that could help you realize that you already have most of what you need? Feeling appreciative of what you have can change what you have in magnificent ways and bring more to be appreciative for into your life. Things you didn't even know you were missing can appear. I am here to introduce you to a new way where you can slowly ease your ego out of the picture, start relying on a new manager to show you where you are blocked and help you tackle all of the issues you have been battling for so long. God can help you realize you don't need more of everything, you need to value others more. In doing so, you will find the path to true happiness. To a peace and joy you thought was unobtainable. God can and will help you find this path if you seek Him.

This book can show you steps you can take to get in touch with your God to open the door to His spirit and let Him in to help you. Don't fall for the self-help lie and buy one more book that advocates how you can fix yourself so you will love yourself. Loving yourself takes work and you might not even know how the ego undermines you at every turn. To gain true self love, you have to examine the past and forgive yourself. Realize you did your best at the time with the knowledge you had and let the past stay in the past. No self-help book will tell you that you are the problem, because your problems make you their number one customer! There's also a problem with self-help books. Your ego is in charge of picking them. It's best logic led you to need one in the first place, now you put it in charge of picking the solution. Why not let the all-knowing God help you pick your next book? This is an anti-self-help book that recommends you get a new manager, and try a new, spiritual approach.

If you want to try this approach, you have to admit that self-reliance isn't working and fire the ego. Ishmael was the sole survivor of the crew led by Captain Ahab in the tale of the insidious fight between Captain Ahab and the great mythical whale, Moby Dick. The tale is a cautionary one of how we can follow our ego blindly, get our lines tangled with the wrong crowd (Captain Ahab) and be led astray. Ishmael was lucky to be the lone survivor of the crew of the Pequod. Do you think when he was delivered from the sea that he signed right up for another tour upon it with an egomaniacal captain in search of the great white whale, Moby Dick?

After I completed the work I am advocating in this book, (by way of the *12 Steps* in the *Big Book* of Alcoholics Anonymous), I stepped out into a new life much different than the one I was living before. I am much happier and have stopped whining about the past and worrying about the future. I feel an inner peace that I had been lacking. Actually things all around me are often crazier than ever, but inside there is this new-found tranquility. The reason is that I placed myself under new management. Now I don't have to worry or fear because I can bring all my crazy issues to my manager and He helps me to see them for what they truly are and to either help me solve them or learn to let go of them! Speaking of letting go, I was recently let go from my job. I'll be honest, I did freak out a little - I got bills after all. But I think God planned this so I would have time to write this book. I hadn't had a sick leave or vacation of more than a couple of days in six years, as I was a contract worker not employee, so both were forced on me. It's been 2 months now and I am doing fine. There is this crazy virus (Corona Virus - ironically) so now getting a job is almost impossible, so I will probably be able to finish this book. My ego wants me to worry, but I am just happily enjoying the free time to read and to write. I am applying for jobs and all but not going overboard and freaking out like the old me would have done.

The pandemic would certainly have been an excellent reason to tie one on in the past! The right job will come when God deems it, so I am being patient. As I said before, I no longer have to rely on myself nor do I want to. I haven't had a drop of alcohol or other drug in almost 3 years now and have no desire to do so. I ask God daily for that wonderful reprieve. My manager runs this show and is the Master of the Universe! He controls everything so why should I worry? Sometimes a bad situation will change right in front of my eyes if I just don't react. Not doing anything is a really awesome strategy I have learned.

Another thing I have found since I put myself under new management is that if there's a book out there I need to read, my manager will lead me to it. He does that often. Also, I can open *any* book and turn to a random page and there will be a message of some type there from my manager. To prove it, I just opened to a random page in Dr. Wayne Dyer's book *The Power of Intention* that is on the table where I am typing. Amazingly the page I randomly opened it to (pg. 225) has this message from Him:

> *"exactly what I need. I pass someone on a walk and they stop to talk. They tell me about a book they're sure I'd love. I jot down the title, look it up, and sure enough, I have what I need.*
>
> *This goes on every day in some way or another as I surrender my ego-mind to the universal mind of intention, and allow precisely the right people to help me with my individual intention. The immediate result of infinite patience is the inner peace that comes from knowing that I have a "senior partner" who will either send me someone, or leave me alone to work it out myself. This is called practical faith, and I urge you to trust in it, be infinitely patient with it, and have an attitude of radical appreciation and awe each time the right person mysteriously appears in your immediate life space." Dr. Wayne Dyer - "The Power of Intention", pg. 225*

I kid you not! This is the kind of stuff I'm talking about. A direct message and always right on point! How can I doubt the perfect job is coming! Now that I have this positive life and all these new-found freedoms, I feel so lucky that I was an alcoholic so I could discover this new design for living from the *Big Book*. Now I see clearly that the work I did in the 12 steps is what allowed me to turn every area of my life over to my new manager and subsequently know this joy and freedom. It saved me from the insanity and futility of reliance on self. I thought my problems were all so unfair and unbeknownst to myself, quietly blamed myself and thought if I managed my life better they wouldn't have occurred! That is insanity! Truthfully bad things do happen here. I can't fix these things, but I can see them through a different lens when I take my ego out of the picture. I can see how staying in the moment and letting them go can help me to be of service to my fellows. My usual disposition now is happy and positive. I no longer hold on to the past, the present is much more exciting!

You don't have to be an alcoholic to have resentments and fears, to screw up relationships, your health, and have a host of financial problems (real or imagined). I can clearly see how the same mistakes I was making before adopting this design for living (even when I was sober) are being made by sober people who have not taken this course. That is why I'm writing this book. My manager said I had to let all the non-alcoholics (normies) know he wanted their attention! He actually woke me up at three in the morning last night and told me to write it down so

I wouldn't forget in the morning! I would complain about the hours he keeps, but He is a really great manager!

So, If you are asking yourself why you picked up this book, I would blame my manager who may want to be your manager! Even if you don't let my manager hire you, if you complete some of the 12 step work included in this book, it could lead to a spiritual awakening and a new understanding and love for yourself. A new gratitude could infuse your life and open the door to a positive and peaceful present that you thought you would never have.

At least it's not another self-help book! It's actually an **"I can't help myself"** book! I wonder what shelf they will put this book on?

Step 1 - Are You Done Yet?

The first step in this re-imagined 12 steps is to admit that you are not living happy, joyous and free. This of course was easy for me because I was unhappy, unjoyous and chained to addiction and to all kinds of negative and insane thoughts. I was desperate to stop drinking, and to want to live again. I didn't know at the time that the Great Spirit of the Universe was trying to contact me. Somehow he had steered me to AA. When I finally found a sponsor, admitting my life was not being managed well was easy. I was done with my way of managing myself - it clearly didn't work, seeing as I was an insane train wreck.

Are you through trying to fix you? Can you admit you may need new management? The first step is to admit it. Let my manager tell you why He needs you and you need Him. If any of these resonate with you, check them.

Tap Into The Power Of God

Here's why God needs you: (Check all that apply)

1. You picked up this book so maybe you need God in your life.
2. The secret is The Creator made only one of you - you are unique. You think you are not unique at all.
3. You don't know how important you are to God. You think you are of no consequence.
4. How can anyone else do the work God put you here to do. You are priceless to Our Creator. You think you are expendable.
5. There have been times when you have been hurt or wronged for no reason, seemingly. You blame God.
6. There have been times when you made the wrong decision and paid the consequences and now you feel guilt or shame and hide this by lashing out at yourself and others, including your Creator.
7. You're mad at God and tell everyone about it but you won't talk to God about it.
8. You have allowed an addiction into your life to replace the hurt, anger or worry you feel.
9. This addiction helps for a moment but it is stealing your joy and your peace of mind, and maybe even killing your spirit slowly.
10. You cannot control this addiction. (drugs, alcohol, smoking, workaholic, junk food, shopping, gambling, pornography etc)
11. Your life has not turned out as you wished and is overly dramatic, complicated, negative or hectic.

12. You push friends or family away and you don't really know why.
13. You watch the news and allow it to make you fearful.
14. You admit you're not doing the best job managing your life.

If you checked more than 7 of the above, you may need a new manager.

If, on the other hand, self-reliance is working out great for you or you don't need a new manager, then the following should be true: (Check all that apply)

1. Your life has turned out exactly as you wished it to be.
2. You never get resentful or hold grudges and you have no fears or worries.
3. You have a fulfilling purpose in life and see how your life makes a difference.
4. You help others.
5. You are happy with your life and don't see need for improvement.

If you checked all 5 of the above, you can put this book down if you want and you probably already know my manager. If you didn't check all 5, my manager would like to talk to you. He says your life should be overflowing and joyful. Will you admit that you don't have all the answers and give Him a chance to show you that He does? Will you admit you can't do everything and be everything and control everything? At least complete the work up to step 6 to prove that you don't need His help. Some of the promises I have found come true for me, that I have listed in Chapter 7 Daily Prescription are:

- You will find freedom in releasing the need for control.
- This freedom will bring you a new-found purpose that will truly satisfy your desires for this life.
- You will lose interest in living in the past or trying to re-arrange the future and find meaning and joy in the ever-evolving present.
- Peace will overcome fear and self-pity will disappear.
- You will begin living a life that is happy, joyous and free.

This was my experience and I hope it will be yours as well.

Are you done letting your ineffectual egomaniac self be in charge yet? If so, all you need to do is agree you may need a new manager. If the answer is *"Yes, I agree that I may need a new manager"*, **Step 1** is done!

Step 2 - Are You Willing To Believe?

Many alcoholics that come to AA don't believe in what the *Big Book* calls a Higher Power or God. Many have been hurt by religion and think this is a religious requirement. Actually, this is a spiritual program not a religious one. The second step basically says you need to believe or *be willing to believe* that there is a **power greater than yourself** in the universe that will help you in your life. So, if you don't believe, I would refer you to something said in many AA meetings "the knowing comes in the doing." This is how it was with me. I did believe in God, but I didn't think God liked me or would help me. I had a chip on my shoulder where God was concerned. However I was willing to admit that I might eventually believe that He could and would help me. In fact I was so desperate for a solution when I got to AA, I hoped against hope that there was a Great Spirit of the Universe that would help me. That hope was my willingness and that was all the willingness that was needed.

Becoming willing to learn about and take steps to contact that Great Spirit of the Universe was easy when I realized that I have taken leaps of faith in other areas of my life in the past. So when I realized self-help wasn't working, why shouldn't I be willing to give the God-idea a try. It doesn't mean I have to join a religion. I just have to be willing to try the next steps, one step at a time. The most compelling part of the argument to me for trying to contact God in this way was the explanation about electricity. We don't know how electricity works, but we use it everyday. We don't really need to understand everything about electricity to use it. God is like this. How can we understand God?

If we need a power greater than ourselves, this does not mean that we are weak. This power is just another source that we can tap into in our daily lives when needed. We don't have to take another's view of this power and call him/her by a certain name - we can decide this for ourselves. The important part is that we be willing to believe in what cannot be seen. The reason this makes sense to me is that I believe in many forces that cannot be seen because science says it is so. Scientists tell us we are made of energy and that matter at it's base is protons and electrons whirling around each other. They can see this with the most powerful microscopes. I can't see this. I can't see electricity. I can't see gravity, but these are forces that affect the world around me and influence me.

I don't insist that I see these forces to believe. Why should I insist that I see God in order to believe He has influence in my world? Our eyes can only see the physical not the metaphysical. They are a sense developed so we can see physical forms. If something is really far away and we can't see it with our own eyes, that doesn't mean it doesn't exist. If something is so small that we can't see it with our eyes, that doesn't mean it doesn't exist. Take a leap of faith and extend your willingness to believe in the unseen to your Creator. In AA I was instructed that I needed to be willing to believe in order to continue the steps.

The successful transformation of so many lives in AA by doing these 12 steps and making a spiritual connection to a higher power is testament that God can defeat some of the most powerful demons we humans will ever face. These were cases that had not been helped by counseling, commitments to institutions or willpower, and these men and women were headed for a jail cell, hospital, asylum or an agonizing alcoholic death. Desperation led them to this program, which led them to a God of their understanding, their own higher power. Attend any open speaker meeting of AA (open meetings are open to the public) and you will hear their inspirational stories. Their willingness to go forward with a spiritually based program, even while not sure exactly what that spirit was and how it could help, has awarded millions of alcoholics with a meaningful, purpose-driven life free of the obsession to drink. Their new lives are testimony to the power of this 12 step solution. We all would like to remain anonymous, but we are out here among you now leading happy, productive, and rewarding lives!

So, are you willing to believe that a new manager could help tackle the problems you are facing and set you on a new and exciting path? My manager would like to show you how much He loves you and is waiting for you to accept His offer. Many alcoholics that were willing to take step 2 continued on to complete the steps and to have this spiritual awakening and are now under new management, as they have testified to in the *Big Book*. Because of their testimonies and those I heard in my AA meetings, I became willing to believe God would help restore me to sanity and finally took Step 2 of the 12 step process that has given me a new design for living. My Manager doesn't think you have to be an alcoholic to work these steps and find Him.

The next part of step 2 is a question that is harder for most to answer because we have to be able to say there is a Great Spirit of the universe with influence in our lives. He either IS or He ISN'T. This question was easy for me to answer as I felt God's influence all around me. I knew that He was there, just didn't understand Him or why He would want to help me. If we say that He ISN'T, then we are saying in effect that we really aren't part of any divine plan we are just here and then we die. No reason. This is what the ego would like for you to believe. Even though I once believed this lie, now this argument makes no sense to me.

If you are agnostic, you are saying God is nothing, there is no reason that we are here and we are not a part of anything bigger. You are alone and you are source. Not only is it vain, but also depressing. If there is a Spirit of the Universe behind it all who has created you, it would also be an ungrateful statement. While I cannot prove, visually, He is, I have ample proof for myself. The years He pursued and persuaded me of His existence time and again, while I struggled for answers that were constantly surrounding me are all the proof I require. Saying "He is everything" is easy for me now, but it is a question you will need to answer eventually. Once again, the knowing sometimes comes in the doing. So the answer to this question may evolve as you complete each step, but you do need to have a willingness to believe to continue on in the steps. Even if it is only a hoped for faith, it is still faith.

If you are *willing to either believe or concede that you might eventually believe* that a power greater than yourself exists and can and will help you, then you have completed Step 2.

Step 3 – If So, Get on Your Knees

So you may know that in AA everyone needs a sponsor. you may know, or think you know what one is from watching "Mom". If not, the job of the sponsor in AA is to walk another alcoholic through the 12 steps and keep tabs on their progress, helping them out when they reach any roadblocks. This means different things to different people in AA . There are many different interpretations of what a sponsor is supposed to do, but to me, the main duties of the sponsor are direction, support and encouragement. From this step on, you will need someone to encourage, support and listen to you. This could be a trustworthy friend or your spouse or anyone you feel will understand that you are taking important steps to try and make conscious contact with a higher power and you need someone who can help keep you motivated and on track. It wouldn't hurt if this is a person who believes in God or in a spiritual lifestyle, but if you don't have anyone like this to turn to, it is not a requirement. You can still do these steps on your own, but a friend who helps keep you motivated to complete the work is important.

The 3rd step is one of the most important because it is a decision to allow God to help you in your life. It is this decision that can make all the difference. In AA, I learned that I was constantly trying to rearrange everything in my world to suit my idea of how it should be. It wasn't working because I wanted control of everything and I had to admit that I am not in control of everything. That was the hardest lesson I have ever had to learn. I learned that running on self-will was constantly putting me on a collision course with others self-will and that letting go of control could actually free me from a great source of pain in my life. If I don't have to arrange my life to suit myself and instead can learn to give that arrangement over to a higher power, I free myself to dream bigger, to enjoy more and to value others more. I learned that some of my biggest dilemmas were not even really any of my business. There is a power behind the scenes that knows where I can best serve my purpose and this purpose gives meaning to my life. I don't have to search for meaning, I can live in it everyday!

I had to give up trying to run the whole show. It wasn't turning out as I planned because the show wasn't mine to run. There were other people (family, friends, co-workers) with their own ideas on how to run the show. Their lives were not subject to my ego's control. Imagine that! When things didn't turn out according to my plan, I felt it was because I didn't try hard enough. So I tried harder and tried to be patient waiting for everyone to follow my plan. They hardly ever did what I wanted them to. I didn't realize how I let something I could never have controlled, the whole show, control me and rob me of my peace and happiness. So when I did finally turn over these day-to-day interactions that were out of my control to a higher power, it was so freeing. I stopped deluding myself that I was in control and let them all go. Letting go is what it is all about. Letting go and letting God.

The 3rd step is where I committed to seeking out this freedom and agreed to give my higher power control while I tried this new way of life. Letting God be my Manager freed up my time. Believe it or not things started actually falling into place and though a lot of the outcomes were not in my plan, they no longer had to be. I saw how living in the present and letting things be as they were actually made me happy, joyous and free. I stopped living in the past and trying to arrange the future and my life improved dramatically. I was able to enjoy the present and it is indeed a gift!

To reach this promise of rebirth, we need to begin a relationship with our higher power. A daily prayer that we can use henceforth to contact God and ask for his will in our life will aid us in reaching out to God each day. This step is where we commit to spend time each day with God and promise to complete the rest of the 12 steps with His help. To complete this third step, the person you choose to help you with the work (sponsor) should be prepared to get down on his/her knees with you and for this first-time recitation, face each other and hold hands. Now recite this prayer together:

"God, I ask you to build a new life with me where my purpose is your will for me. Clear my mind of selfish thoughts which lead to self-destruction. Make me a beacon of light shining your Truth in this world. Place someone in my path today that I might help with wisdom, patience and love."

Note: If you are still social-distancing due to the Corona Virus, you can remain 6 feet apart and skip the hand holding or even use face-time but do get on your knees!

By taking this step with a witness, you are making a contract with God and you agree to finish the rest of the work involved in the 12 steps and to pass this knowledge on to others. You have completed Step 3.

Daily Prescription

You are now beginning step 4, which involves self examination and reflection. Read this chapter (*Chapter 7: Daily Prescription*) everyday from this step forward and follow the directions in it everyday.

Synopsis - each day we start the day on our knees, and we recite the 3rd step prayer found at the end of the last chapter. Then we ask God for guidance and meditate on the day to come. Last, we review our day with a special emphasis on improving over time.

First we start with the prayer from the 3rd step:

> *God, I ask you to build a new life with me where my purpose is your will for me. Clear my mind of selfish thoughts which lead to self-destruction. Make me a beacon of light shining your Truth in this world.*

> *Place someone in my path today that I might*
> *help with wisdom, patience and love.*

We ask God for guidance during the day. We thank Him for our blessings both those we have now and those that are to come. We ask Him to show us His will for us and help us to be of service to those people he places in our path today. There are some more specific prayers in Appendix I that you can utilize daily. Then we meditate for at least 10 minutes. Please try the guided meditations for "Gods Pharmacy" in Appendix II while you are reading and doing the work in this book. These meditations are in audio format on youtube under Danielle C. Pace. These meditations are meant to help you to tap into God's strength all day long and can be used anytime one is needed. I usually choose 2 of them I think I will need during the day for my morning meditation, then do another at night to relax me before I sleep. Then we read the **Daily Reading** below. You may break up the daily reading to Morning, As Needed, and Night if you would like.

Daily Reading: (Morning)

After our morning devotion we contemplate our plans for the day and ask God for his guidance throughout the day. We vow to consult him in all of our dilemmas and to use our God-given intuition when facing indecision. We do not have to make snap decisions and we do not have to control everyone and everything. We may simply say "God's will be done" and pray or meditate if a decision is required. We will surely see that our motives change when we are trying to make decisions that agree with our new-found purpose and God's will for our life.

After using this approach for awhile, we find ourselves more able to make hard decisions and also to let go when no action is required. We learn to trust our intuition and to seek God throughout the day. We also learn to "pause" and do a quick consult with our higher power rather than take on problems that are none of our business. We learn to let go and we learn to let God.

During the day when Needed:

We admit that we are no longer running the show. We repeat the short serenity prayer below when needed during the day and use our pause button when necessary.

> Serenity Prayer: "*God grant me the serenity to accept the things I cannot change, the courage to change the things I can, and the wisdom to know the difference.*" – Reinhold Niebuhr

(Nightly)

Each night we constructively review our day. We look for instances where we were selfish, unsure, resentful or unkind. We examine what fears may have driven our behavior and how we could have sought help from our higher power instead of acting from a point of self. Notice the word constructively above. We do not blame ourselves.

This is a healing process. We ask for guidance from God if a similar situation arises in the future. We congratulate ourselves for instances where we used intuition to pause and respond in a loving way even in the midst of chaos. Our purpose is evolving and so are we.

We are working towards a promising new future where we have tackled our most vexing problems and are free to create and enjoy a bright future. This is how we will begin to live happy, joyous and free. Here is a list of promises that I believe you will begin to experience during this 12 step process:

- You will learn what things really are your business and what is indeed out of your control.
- You will find freedom in releasing the need for control.
- This freedom will bring you a new-found purpose that will truly satisfy your desires for this life.
- You will lose interest in living in the past or trying to rearrange the future and find meaning and joy in the ever-evolving present.
- Peace will overcome fear and self-pity will disappear.
- You will have a new manager to guide you and you will find that God is the driving force behind your new design for living.
- You will begin living a life that is happy, joyous and free.

Resentments and Fears

The next 2 steps (Steps 4 and 5) will be dealing with the biggest threats to your happiness and usefulness, resentments and fears. If you do this work and see where your resentments originate, you will begin to understand why your thought-life is so important. You will understand the law of attraction that has been shaping your life. You will comprehend why your fears will turn into defenses and your defenses into self-fulfilling prophesies, and if you reach an understanding of how you set this process in motion with your fearful thoughts, you can change your thoughts and change the outcome. Your whole outlook on life will change.

In AA, the way to bring other alcoholics into AA is by attraction not promotion. I was told by others in AA that I would need to get a sponsor to help me through the steps. I was told that I would know her when I met her because she would have something I wanted. I would be attracted to her. I hemmed and hawed and didn't pick a sponsor. One day I was in a bookstore and some random guy came up to me and handed me a book and said "This is the book you are looking for!" Then he walked away. I thought "Who does that?" It was a book called "The Magic" by Rhonda Byrne. I bought the book because, well because I thought "that was definitely divine intervention!" The book advocates a 28 day course in gratitude. Each day is a different lesson including lessons on relationships, health, and finances. It lays down a solid basis for gratitude's affect and the law of attraction.

It was shortly after finishing the lessons in this book that a friend and I were searching for an AA meeting and got lost. We were in the complete wrong part of town, but we did see people going into a building and realized that it was an AA meeting, so we pulled over and went inside. It just happened to be a celebrant anniversary meeting and all of the AAers with anniversaries that month were giving speeches. As we sat there, a cute little wisp of a girl got up and told her story.

She grew up in LA, the typical hippy girl, sex, drugs and rock and roll. She told how her father was an alcoholic and took her to AA meetings with him and she thought she would never abuse alcohol, but eventually she did. She said that this was her 4 year sober anniversary! She talked about how great life was now being sober. She found and married the perfect guy, has a career where people pay to fly her to other countries to take pictures. She's a professional photographer! I was so attracted to her positive attitude and adventurous spirit. I asked her to be my sponsor after the meeting and she agreed! I feel like this was also divine intervention because we stumbled on this meeting looking for a different one, but it was no accident. I was meant to meet her and to be part of the fellowship there. The people in this group are all like family to me now and I know this blessing came to me because of doing the gratitude work prescribed in *"The Magic."* If you lookup what the **law of attraction means** on google, it states

> *"The law of attraction is the attractive, magnetic power of the Universe that draws similar energies together. It manifests through the power of creation, everywhere and in many ways. Even the law of gravity is part of the law of attraction. This law attracts thoughts, ideas, people, situations and circumstances."*

Wow, that is a powerful law. To me it says positivity attracts positivity and negativity attracts negativity. In this world, there is both good and bad, positive and negative. In the book *"The Magic"* I was introduced to this law of attraction. Feeling grateful attracted more situations in which I could feel grateful! Your mind is a very powerful and connected tool. When most people hear this, they don't believe it. What is the alternative? The mind is a mass of protoplasm, totally unconnected to anything, a temporary thinking machine that will turn to dust when you die? That's what I thought before I read the "Magic", but that book taught me to see there is some other force out there working based on our thoughts and feelings. In the book *"The Secret"*, also *by Rhonda Byrne*, it tells you to do a little test to see the law of attraction working in your life. Concentrate on something small and see if you can bring it into your life. Really feel that thing in your hands. I thought okay, why not? So I concentrated for a little bit on a red hibiscus flower, then forgot about it. A few days later, my friend and I were early to a meeting and there was a gentleman there who said "I picked 2 flowers to give to the first 2 ladies who show up and here you are!" The one he gave me was a red hibiscus flower! I got chills. That was powerful proof to me as I held that flower in my hand. I hadn't told anyone about my little test! No simple thinking machine without a connection to *something greater* could do this. There is more at work. There is some link to a source of more and infinite power which link can be reached by our minds.

Have you ever predicted a good or bad outcome? Researches are finding now that when they observe something, the very act of their observation can change the outcome of what they are observing. How? Could our thoughts or expectations of what will happen change outcomes? I am one who believes this to be true. This is why fear is such a powerful predictor and can skew outcomes. Have you ever been really worried about something, prepared for the worst and thought you had it totally covered and you were protected? Then that very thing happens and it turns out you didn't have it totally covered? There was something you hadn't thought of?

Isn't this the law of attraction at work? All of your fear and all of your preparing and all of your best defenses are actually working to bring that situation into being and even more powerfully than you had feared it would be.

Instead you need to release the fear and make no defenses against it. But how do you do this? That is what the work in the 4th step aims to help you understand. The goal is to point your attention to the root cause of all your resentments and fears your thinking! (In AA we call it "stinking thinking"). If you want to get rid of resentments and not build new ones, then you need to examine this stinking thinking thoroughly. I never understood that my biggest problems with people, institutions and even ideas were caused by my fears and all my defensive thoughts and actions against them until I did the work in the 4th step. I gradually realized that fear is a very powerful thought and extremely magnetic. The more you fear, the more fear you will produce and the more fearful you will become. Stop the vicious cycle immediately. Reclaim your thoughts and reclaim your peace of mind.

There is a popular acronym for fear ("False Evidence Appearing Real"). This is exactly what fear is. You see it on the news every night. The worst things always lead. The negative things seem to be the most important! That's so we can all go out and spread fear. I've always thought someone might be out there manipulating the stock market by creating fearful stories, then getting rich. I don't know if it's true, but it's reason enough for me not to be a participant. If you're trying to keep your thoughts positive, how on earth is watching bad news going to help? Isn't the truth that none of us are really in control? Like the movie *"Final Destination"*, when it is time for us to go, we will. None of us will get out of here alive (our bodies anyway). Also, there is plenty of good news out there that never gets reported. Wouldn't you rather hear that in your short adventure here? If there is good news it's hardly ever the lead story. Do an experiment and try not watching the first 10 minutes of the news. When the weatherman comes on, usually the worst and most sensational is over. Now you will get informative news. What the weather will be like over the next couple of days and usually some feel good story at the end. See how much more positive you feel after a week of this.

A positive attitude is going to be important to maintain while you do the 4th step work in the next chapter. The 4th step entails a lot of writing and self-examination. It is the hardest step to get through. In AA this step is what derails most attempts to complete the 12 steps, but the result of this work is a new freedom through understanding and totally worth it. Don't miss out on the blessings that await on the other side of this step. This step is the foundation of the rest of the steps after it. Make sure to do a thorough self-examination so you have a strong cornerstone on which to place the remaining steps.

In the Big Book, it talks about resentments and about how alcoholics are self-centered and ego-centric. Even when we put down the drink, these qualities are still there. This is what in AA we call a "dry drunk". To conquer this ego-centric problem requires extreme self-examination. Many of us don't want to do this. I believe we all have the tendency to think we are not self-centered or ego-centric, but how do you know if you don't examine your past and tackle resentments you feel towards others? Did your ego play a part in your past and present resentments? Is it playing a part in your current dilemmas? Is it causing certain problems now that are robbing you of your peace? Step 4 and Step 5 will help you to see through the smoke screen raised by your ego to keep you in the dark about its plans for you.

One of my favorite lines from the Big Book of Alcoholics Anonymous is found on page 62 and goes like this:

> *"Driven by a hundred forms of fear, self-delusion, self-seeking, and self-pity, we step on the toes of our fellows and they retaliate."*
> *Big Book of Alcoholics Anonymous - pg. 62*

That is what the 4th step aims to show you in a nut-shell. Why do you do things that cause others to retaliate? If you are like me, you think "Oh I never do anything like that", trust me we all do. The 4th and 5th steps will open your eyes and change your whole perspective. Your motivations, when revealed will help you see any fear laden or ego-driven behaviors and allow you to change them into positive affirmative behaviors in the future.

Step 4 - Examine Your Past Fearlessly

Unlike the previous 3 steps, Step 4 is no simple task. This is you asking God to help you identify your past and present resentments and list your subsequent actions as well as examining your fears to see what is sabotaging your present peace and happiness. To do this, we need to reevaluate our motives and our actions and reexamine the fears that played a part in their development. This examination will help us avoid future resentments. What did I really want to happen? Examining this requires God's help, which is why it is important that we read and follow instructions in *Chapter 7 "Daily Prescription"* every day.

This step is basically an inventory of all your resentments and fears. Resentments sabotage your happiness and keep you from moving forward fearlessly to the peaceful place promised in Step 9. Looking back on these resentments without resolving and releasing them projects them into the future and fear seals and locks them into a self-fulfilling prophesy that dooms you to repeat them. Through a thorough examination of their root cause, you will begin to see a pattern and understand why you must release them. You will comprehend why self-reliance fails you during these times and why you need new management.

Doing this step is how I finally came to understand how to conquer my ego. It was controlling my happiness and stopping the flow whenever I got to a new level where I should have felt peace. It would start with fearful thoughts and then demand I make some defense so I would be protected. It all seemed so logical, and the fear so real at the time but, in hindsight, I see how it robbed me of peace and joy time and again. I was lucky to get into an AA Ladies group that used a very thorough 4th step procedure similiar to the procedure below to root out ego-centric behavior and allow me to see past my Ego's manipulations of the truth.

In AA we have an acronym for ego. It is "Edging God Out". Another one I have heard is "Everyone's Greatest Obstacle." I think both apply. The ego will tell you that you don't need anyone and it will try to isolate you. It will tell you how unfair life is and that God must not exist or he really doesn't like you. It will tell you that you can control outcomes if only everyone around you will cooperate. When will that ever happen? It will convince you that you can run the show and make a great life. But the ego knows there will always be someone or something that will not cooperate with your plan. The ego knows what you want and tells you as soon as you get it that it is not enough. The ego is the reason you have not been able to find happiness here, unless it is short-lived. The connection to a higher positive force is what you are missing. During this step, we need to check our ego at the door. A detailed description of how to do this work is below, but first let me describe what the work entails.

The first 2 parts of this step are to list all of the people, institutions and principles that we have had resentments against in our past and give the reasons. Then we must look honestly at 4 questions we have for each resentment. These questions and their answers contain clues to unlocking the door to allow Spirit in and slam the door on the EGO moving forward.

The next part is to examine our fears and how we set the ball rolling by believing in them. The examination of how our self-reliance fails us in these times is another key to tap into Spirit in this part of the work.

Lastly we examine our relationships and how we have used our sexuality in the past to influence others. We ask God for a new perspective on relationships. We create a "God letter" describing what we would most like to see in our future most personal relationship.

During this work, the ego will fight for itself and throw obstacles in your path, trying to convince you this work is meaningless and you can run the show if you just try harder. It will strive to convince you that you are right and someone else is wrong. As soon as you start judging someone else, and thinking you know more than they do, you will know that your ego is taking control. I was lucky enough to have two wonderful sponsors to help me through this step and both times they kept me on track. Call someone if you are struggling during this work and don't listen to your ego. You need to be painstakingly focused to complete this work. Remember you are working to reach the sunshine of the spirit and the promises in your daily prescription. That is why you made the contract with God in the 3rd step. You promised to complete this work and pass it on. Believe me, once you truly get this, you will want to pass it on.

INSTRUCTIONS:

First, buy 2 spiral notebooks for this work.

During the following work, devote one hour each day to writing. Start the session with the prayer from the 3rd step and ask God to help you with the work.

Part 1: (Resentment List)

In the first notebook, make a list of people, institutions or principles where you have built a resentment. This is the resentment list. Try to include all names of your past and present resentments, and number the entries. Don't put the reason yet, just write the names. Ask God to help you if you get stuck and can't remember some. Make sure to put yourself and God on this list. Do not start the next part until this part is complete.

Part 2: (Resentment Causes)

In the same notebook, for each of the names above, make a separate page with the number of the resentment, and the name and the cause of the resentment at the top of the page. If you have multiple resentments for a single person, pick the top 3 and make a separate page for each resentment (a, b, c). I have found that if you list the top 3 resentments, you will cover most of the reasons for the resentments against this person. This will make your life easier when you get to the next part of the work. Do not start the next part until this part is complete.

Part 3: (Resentment Questions)

For each of the pages in Part 2 where you have written the name and the resentment at the top of the page, add the numbers 1 - 4 with some space in-between to answer. Next follow the instructions below to answer the questions for the resentment listed at the top of the page.

Question 1: What did I want? (Where was I selfish?) I wanted - (only 1 answer):

Examples: a better friend, a caring relationship, a loving mother, an exciting time, an appreciative boss, a kind coworker, a trusting boyfriend, financial help, unconditional love, a respectful relationship, better communication, control, supervision, to be valued, to be loved, to be respected, to be right, sympathy, to win, to be the best, to be rescued, security, x person to do x, etc.

Question 2: What was the truth? (Where was I dishonest?)

The truth is - (as many as you want):

We will circle back to this question after we complete Part 6.

For now just add the number 2 and leave some blank lines.

Question 3: What were my actions?

Here's what I did to get what I wanted - (as many as you want):

Now describe your self-seeking behaviors. What you did to try to get what you wanted or what you did because you didn't get what you wanted. **You can put multiple answers.** Examples: argued, criticized, attacked, silent treatment, shutdown, sarcastic, cried, built a grudge, flirted, lied, played the victim, became powerless, humiliated them, talked behind their back, defiant, sulking, passive aggressive, judging, became violent, manipulate with guilt, failed to confront, enlisted others, people pleasing, compromised beliefs, avoidance, addiction, etc.

Question 4: What was I afraid of losing, not getting, or happening?

I was afraid of - (only 1 answer):

Here pick the #1 underlying fear that not getting or losing what you wanted in Question 1 above is. **Only 1 answer.** Examples: losing friendship, abandonment, not being good enough, being powerless, disapproval, being wrong, admitting mistakes, family being hurt, not being appreciated, not being trusted, being dependent, being abused, not being respected, punishment, losing my job, losing my family, financial hardship, etc.

Do not start the next part until this part is complete.

Part 4: Fear Inventory

In the second notebook make a list of the fears you listed down in Question 4 (from **Part 3 Resentment Questions**). Combine any that seem to be the same thing with different wording. For example not being perfect, not being good enough and not being a good Mom might be lumped together as not being good enough. After you have the list narrowed down, make your fears list. Number and list the fears so you have a reference. Now, in the second notebook create a separate page for each fear, with the number and fear listed at the top of the page. Add the numbers 1 - 4 with some space in-between to answer. Next follow the instructions below to answer the questions for the fear listed at the top of the page.

Question 1: Where did the fear originate?

What was the first time you experienced the fear or an example of when you experienced the fear?

Question 2: How did you attempt to control the fear

What did you do to control the fear? You can refer back to Question 3 of the turnarounds where you listed actions you did to get or did because you didn't get what you wanted.

Question 3: Why my strategy failed and I built a resentment

A. How did self-reliance (Question 2) fail me?

B. How did I set the ball rolling?

C. What happened as a result?

Question 4. What could I do instead?

Write this sentence first:

"I could trust and rely on God to remove the fear of xxx and direct my attention to what he would have me be."

Writing this sentence over and over for every fear will help you to remember in the future that fear is to be given to God, not handled by you. You just have to BE in faith, you don't have to DO anything!

Now write a sentence or sentences in your own words that explains how you can trust and rely on God **instead of yourself** in any future situation where this fear arises.

Some examples: If something is out of my control or none of my business, I could pray about the situation and give it to God instead of being fearful. I can ask God to remove the fear. I can trust God to help me overcome the fear. I could be more thankful for what I already have and trust God instead of fearing I will lose it. I could ask God to help me be more grateful towards others instead of being envious and ungrateful. I could stay out of situations that are not my business and let God handle them. I can try to be myself (the person God created me to be) instead of pretending to be someone else to please others. I can pray to God over the situation that is making me fearful and release resentments I have made because of the fear (forgiveness).

Do not start the next part until this part is complete.

Part 5: Sex Inventory

In the same notebook, ask yourself where you might have used sexuality or manipulation to try to get what you wanted.

Create a list of people (name or description)

For each of the above on a separate page answer these 4 questions:

A. Conduct - brief (affair, flirt, one-night stand, cried, manipulated etc)

B. Was it selfish - Yes or No

C. Was it dishonest or Inconsiderate - Yes or No

D. What should I have done instead? (ex. left them alone, acted like a lady/gentleman, said no, had more confidence, been honest, been kind) Do not start the next part until this part is complete.

Part 6: God Letter

Write a letter to God describing what you would want your ideal partner relationship to most look like

This letter is important whether you are in a relationship or not. A bad relationship can be changed to a good one if you are willing to work at it with a positive mind set. Put forth the positive attributes you would like to see in your partner and skip any ones that are negative (i.e. don't put stop nagging - instead put peaceful or soothing). You are attempting to attract a positive relationship not a negative one, so try to use only positive words. Make sure to thank God in advance for the wonderful outcome he will be helping you to attain in your current or future relationship.

If you have completed the above work, congratulations! You now have a better sense of why your fears play a part in resentments and you can now go back to your resentments question list and answer question 2 - What was the truth for each of your resentments.

What was the truth? Here are some of the answers you could use for **Question 2 what was the truth? select as many as you want:** I had no control, it wasn't my business, not expressing feelings, I didn't care, I presented false info, I cheated, I lied, I created jealousy, I felt inferior, I felt justified, I omitted something, I thought I knew best, half-truths, I was jealous, I was angry, people-pleasing, etc.

If you have either "to" or "be" in the answer for Question 1, then probably the truth is it is something out of your control or none of your business. Why do we try to control things that are out of our control or none of our business? I'm not sure but I do know I did a lot of it and it doesn't work. It will always lead to disappointment and probably to a resentment. Let other people be who they are. It is between them and their creator. It is none of your business whether they like you either. They will like you or not so why build a resentment? Don't you want to be who you were created to be? Stop trying to people-please. Another person may like you or not. That is their business not yours. Do not make other people change to suit you. Let them be who they are and accept them or release them. Wouldn't it be boring if everyone here was just like you? Celebrate the differences and try to understand other's point of view. You may just grow your own mind in the process! Have you ever heard the phrase "opposites attract"? There is a reason God puts people in your life. He wants to expand your horizons. You may be sent to help them or they may be sent to help you.

Did you want someone to do something and they didn't, or did they do something you didn't like? Who is in control of them - you or them? Why build a resentment or retaliate when whatever they did is basically their problem, not yours. If it caused you to lose something you thought you had, then maybe God has a purpose for you that required you to lose it. The truth is you couldn't control others actions if you wanted to, so you have to trust that whatever they did even if it is unknowingly done by them out of spite, is part of God's plan to prosper you. Looking for a silver lining is always the correct response as God is working behind the scenes to show you your purpose and to strengthen your resolve.

Think about what you wanted and then look at what you did. If you wrote that you wanted "a better friend", were your actions those of a good friend? Maybe you built a grudge and pushed them away. Is that what a good friend would do? Did you fear losing their friendship and ultimately lose it by your actions? Do you see how your ego took charge? Did it help? I went through all of my resentments one by one and looked at my actions and fears. I found that my actions were usually in defense against something I feared and not in offense for something I valued. They were ego-driven. The truth is in every one of my resentments I should have played offense and told the defensive ego to return to the dugout. I examined what I valued about the person I had the resentment against. When I looked up each fear in my fear inventory there was a positive solution that I could have implemented in every case that would most certainly have yielded better results and been more in line with my values, not my ego's.

If you are like me, this work has opened your eyes. You should have begun to sense the flow of the spirit into you during this work. Be on the lookout for little revelations about yourself and how much you are loved. When you first connect to this positive spirit, you may think you are going crazy, but trust me it is just that you are now part of a large positive network that can make things happen. Good things. You have been connected to negativity for so long while guilt, shame and fear have kept your ego at the helm. You are replacing these with knowledge of your innate goodness. This newfound love for yourself will help you remove your inner egomaniac from power. You are beginning to understand how worry about the future is futile and can actually harm you. Are you willing to let the past be the past and move on to be entirely present in the present? Are you ready to stop projecting the past into your present and future? Let's put our team up to bat and start playing offense.

The sex inventory should have shown you how your search for love was actually a self-reliance and defensive disaster in most cases. Everybody wants a great partner by their side but expecting good results from wily tactics doesn't work. Trying to manipulate another with flirting, jealousy or guilt will only yield temporary results and harm a precious relationship in the long run. Trying to be someone you are not to please someone else is not maintainable. Being who you are is important while you grow into the wonderful person God has prepared for you to be. If you need a partner on this journey, treat him/her with respect, be yourself, and choose wisely. Make sure it is someone who is working and growing alongside you. Look carefully at the last question and try to remember what you should do instead the next time you contemplate using wiles to manipulate another.

How did you feel writing the God letter? When I wrote mine I realized that since I have begun to love myself, I found myself including the phrase "like me" often in my God letter. I wrote a list of positive attributes I would like in a partner and for instance I wrote "He should like to sing in the car, like me. He should like dancing, like me." Wow, now I was finally picking important things for a relationship, not "a nice car" or "a good job". Those things can change, but the things you like to do together are more important and a better predictor of happiness. Once you begin to love yourself, you won't want to be anyone else but yourself. This God letter opened my eyes to the possibility of actually finding a mate which I had pretty much given up on. I kept wondering why I chose the same egomaniac guy every time. It was because I was an egomaniac! I was trying to be somebody I never could live up to because I didn't like myself. Now I know that I can be my goofy self with better results. Now that I love myself, I want someone to love me for me. I want someone who will show me their true self and walk with me towards a positive future we can enjoy together! Someone who knows that this life is to be enjoyed and who isn't fearful and judgmental.

After I finished my God letter, I created a vision board where I cutout pictures of happy couples enjoying their lives together and pasted them on poster board. It included some of the activities I wanted to do with my future partner and words to describe our relationship.

This isn't required, but to me writing the God letter without showing God my vision would be like building a house but not painting the walls and adding furniture. I want to move in to my house, not just look at it! I wanted God to see what my ideal relationship would look like. Vision boards are a technique I learned by reading "The Secret" and they really work. Basically a vision board is cutouts or pictures of things you would like to do or see pasted on a piece of poster board. A friend of mine had a bunch of words on hers and I had a bunch of pictures on mine. Lately I have been incorporating words with my pictures as well and this helps to evoke feelings when looking at the board. I try to look at mine daily.

Spend a little time contemplating your 4th step work. In our next step we will review this work with God and another and make some admissions regarding it.

Step 5 - Admit the Truth

Let's pour cement into the foundation that you have set in place with your previous steps.

In AA during the 5th step we meet and review our 4th step work with our sponsor or another understanding person and we invite God into the discussion. Admitting that we played a role in creating and maintaining our resentments is crucial to finally being able to let them go and give up self-reliance (selfish reliance) and hire God as our new manager. If you have not yet chosen a "sponsor" that you can review these notebooks with, you will now need to find someone to do this step with. If you are comfortable telling someone you know about your resentments and what part you played in them, then invite that person to spend time reviewing the work with you. If you aren't comfortable talking with someone you know, please find someone you don't know. Perhaps a psychologist or an acquaintance you feel would be closed-mouthed and understanding. Try to choose someone who will be non-judgmental and who will help you see that your actions were driven by an out of control ego and nothing to feel guilt or shame over. Make sure it is someone you trust to keep your admissions confidential. This step may take several sessions as you will be going over all of the work you did in the 4th step. Make sure the person you choose is aware of this commitment. You can break it down to 1 or 2 hour sessions as necessary. This step does not need to be done in one day and probably cannot be done in one day.

This step is important because during your discussions about this work, you will be releasing the shame and guilt that the ego would like you to carry for eternity. Nothing would serve the ego more than for you to live in the past, continually feeling sorry for yourself, shameful, angry, or jealous and bitter. Beating yourself up for every imagined mistake you or someone else has ever made is what the ego does best. Believe me there is no time machine to allow you to go back and change your actions and who is to say if some worse fate might have arisen if you did. Just watch *"Back to the Future II"*. Why waste time on the past? Every minute you do robs your present and subtracts from your future. Let it go! That is the purpose of the 5th step. By admitting your past mistakes to God, to yourself and to another, you are banishing the shame and bitterness your ego would like you to hold on to forever. You are laying a firm foundation where you can let go of the past, release fear and build a new and fabulous life.

To do this step correctly, all you need do is review your 4th step work with another and invite God into the discussion by saying the prayer from the 3rd step before you begin. In AA we add an extra chair in the room for God. Be prepared for a long talk. Read this chapter aloud with the other person before starting your first session of the 5th step. How we do it in AA is one person will read a couple of paragraphs then the other will read a couple and so on. Most people will understand and be glad to help you release these issues in the way this chapter recommends. Another perspective besides your ego's is important as the person you are discussing your resentments with has none of the biases the ego has created in your mind. Try to withhold nothing during this discussion. Go page by page through your 2 notebooks. You are now examining the origin of past resentments so you will be able to release them. You are reviewing your inventory of fears. You are admitting self-reliance has failed you in mitigating circumstances and should now know and admit how self-reliance will always fail you at these times. Go over your fears and be truthful about the part your fears played in your resentments. Talk about your God letter and what you want to bring to and see in your future most personal relationship.

When you sit down with God and someone else to discuss your work, you will be taking a deep dive into your motives for past resentments. The first turnaround question - "What did you want?" is crucial. It is a clue to the ego's power over you. Looking back, we tend to think we had altruistic motives. I just wanted a better friend, but truthfully most times I wanted to be right or I wanted more control over another person, or I wanted to be respected and I felt disrespected. I wanted someone to do something that they did not do. I wanted to control outcomes for me and those around me, and was angered when others interfered. For me, there were many control issues that my ego masked as altruistic motives. The truth in most of these cases is **It was none of my business** or **The situation was out of my control**! I damaged many relationships by listening to my ego tell me to **control a situation that was none of my business**. Over and over as I discussed my supposed motives with my sponsor, I realized the truth was **I had no control and felt powerless** in most of the situations where I had built resentments. My ego had made sure to make the situation worse by forcing me to act in counter-productive ways to assure my fear would be realized. Over and over again the pattern repeated. This examination opened my eyes! Every time I would tell my sponsor what I had answered for question 1. What I wanted, and the things I had done in question 3. to get what I wanted, she would look at me and say *"No that couldn't be what you wanted!"* She helped me realize that **what I had really wanted at the time was clouded by my ego.** I did not even know what I really wanted! The truth had been masked by the fears that my ego had told me I could control. This forced me to really examine my motives and my fear driven behavior! I could now admit the fear wasn't even real. Looking back, I see the carnage I left behind. It was mind-boggling how many times these simple patterns repeated themselves. This amazing woman gave me the gift of truth and now I understand the phrase "The truth shall set you free" It really has!

While doing this step, you may have revelations about yourself because your contact with God is being firmly established. Don't be surprised if forgiving yourself finally is within reach. You will come to understand that you did the best you could with the knowledge that you had at the time and your overreliance on self. You will release many of the fears by realizing you really can't control most of the things you want to, nobody can. **Also, Our perspective of situations can change the situations.** When you realize you have no control of other people's opinions, somehow their opinions lose power over you! When you realize you can't control other people's actions, you will stop trying to! You can't control other peoples' outcomes either. A lot of times you can't even control your own outcomes. And the truth is that bad things do happen to good people in this world and God wants you to realize that **He is in control and there is a reason for everything**. While it is hard for us to see the big picture, it is not hard for God. His will is always in your best interest whether it seems like it at the time or not. I realize now that during some of the hardest times I ever went through God was there with me and trying to reach out to me to help me **change my perspective and realize I could reach out to Him**.

I had been carrying around a resentment against my old boss. Then I lost that job. Losing that job was the catalyst that brought a much better job where I could be valued. So now, looking back I am glad that something didn't feel right at my old job. Reaching out to God and having faith that another job was coming allowed my life to change in magnificent ways. I would have trudged along at my old job if I hadn't been let go so God sent some circumstance to change things up. God wants us to know Him and trust Him. Someone who doesn't know God is said to be agnostic. What is the definition of agnostic? Not knowing!

The truth is you are a valuable part of God's plan and his love for you is never-ending. He wants you to **know** this. He only made one of you, then he broke the mold. He wants what is ultimately in your best interest. There may be only one way to get you to the place where you can be in total fulfillment of His plans for you and there may be hardships along that path. These may be necessary hardships as the path to overcoming them is where you will forge your faith and learn to be of service to others in the future. These hardships may be how you will find your purpose. With the proper perspective, these challenges can be overcome and seen in hindsight as lessons learned. There will also be hard decisions. He knows the big plan. Seek His help when you don't know which road to take. We can't see the parts of the plan that involve others. He can. He wants a relationship where you know Him and seek Him daily. He needs your input to shape your destiny and those of others around you. You are but a part of the whole story.

This step is not about feeling guilt and shame over your past actions, it is about letting the past go and not projecting it into your future. Stop beating yourself up. You could not have known how sneaky your ego was. Realize that you did play a part in past resentments. Examining that part will help you to build a better tomorrow where you won't have to build more resentments. It is about a commitment to release fears and ineffectual defenses your ego has made against them. Instead trust in God and your relationship with him. **Allow yourself to be totally present in all your present moments.** Fear and worry for the future is a waste of time and detracts from your joy in the present. Trust God, stop building defenses and start living offensively one day at a time. Start loving all and allowing them to have their own opinions. Their opinion of you is their business not yours.

Going over your resentment list, fears and sex inventory with another will help you to see that certain behaviors in the past did not serve you well in the long run. Looking at this objectively, you will probably see a pattern of like actions emerge. I know I did. The very thing I was fearing was what my actions were bringing about. Mostly my actions were defensive and I wasn't acting in a loving and optimistic way. Feeling negatively about a situation can lead you to limit your options to negative ones. Saying the prayer from the 3rd step every morning and asking God to help you in all the trials of the day will change your attitude from negative to positive. **Being thankful first thing in the morning is very important.** The tone you set for your day and knowing that you will be given inspiration, if needed, allows you to not act impulsively.

During the day, if you feel negatively about something, hit the pause button and decide not to take any action. I have found that when I do this, I will eventually find some sort of silver lining in the whole situation which will give me a positive action that I can take to improve the situation. It is hard in the moment because usually someone is presenting you with a problem and expecting you to make an impulsive decision, an immediate response. Don't be intimidated. Just say you need time to think about it. Usually you really do need time to think about it. Some of my worst mistakes were split second decisions or ones made when I was in no shape to make any decisions. Now I know I don't have to act impulsively if I don't want to. I can ask God to direct me. It is harder to go back and fix a mistake than to not make one in the first place, so hit pause and take time to do a quick consult before you respond.

In the 5th step, you are making a choice to look objectively at the way you did things in the past. When I saw my pattern, the importance of reading the daily prescription became obvious. Getting on my knees every morning and being thankful, saying prayers and meditating is part of my routine, so I rarely forget, but when I do and I sense everything falling apart for the day, I immediately bow down and start the day over. Checking in with the boss first thing every day always gets us on the same page! This is the cement that holds my new found freedom in place. It is a re-affirmation daily that my ego is not running the show today! The ego will chip away at any holes you leave in your resolve. That is why the Daily Prescription advocates reviewing your day, constructively, at the end of each day. This is not destructively. You are trying to improve your life so be constructive. By doing this, you will be able to see immediately if the ego is re-asserting control. By keeping the fear inventory notebook close, you can see the positive advice for the particular fears which crop up that day, and reassess your actions. Did you mess up? No big deal, learn from it. Believe me you will mess up. When you do, go fix it. Be loving and be kind.

Read your God Letter out loud and really picture this being fulfilled in your life. If you are looking for a relationship, this will help guide you to a positive relationship. If you are currently in a relationship, this can improve it. By being grateful for the positive things in your partner, the positive things will increase. Try to ignore the negative things. This may be hard, but the negative things will decrease the less you concentrate on them and make defenses against them. The law of attraction will reward your positivity with positive outcomes. Take your God Letter out occasionally and re-read it. Remember you are asking for God's assistance so be sure to thank him in advance for the great relationship!

After this discussion, you should finally be able to release any shame and guilt over your past actions. You should be able to release the resentment as well. You will realize God is on your side and wants to help you improve. You will begin to sense you are on the right path and walking hand in hand with the Great Spirit of the Universe. In AA we say that you are becoming God-conscious.

After completing the 5th Step, your sponsor should place your hand in God's hand and say that you are now in a partnership and he is your new Manager.

Find a place where you can be quiet for an hour. Meditate and thank God that you now know him better. Thank Him for revealing your past ego-driven behaviors. Thank Him for showing you how you can trust and rely on Him who knows all in the future when fear overtakes you. Thank Him for the knowledge that in the future you can hit pause and most of the problems you encounter during your day do not have to be solved by you. You don't have to do anything as most things are out of your control or none of your business anyway! If you need help, ask your manager. If someone else needs help, help them if you can, but pray or refer the person to your manager if they are insisting upon your help and you know it is something out of your control. You are no longer running the show! Admit it and be glad!

When you are through meditating, do a self-review of your work in these first five steps. After devoting time for meditating and review, carefully read and answer these first 5 questions:

1. Are you done yet?
2. Are you willing to believe?
3. Did you get on your knees?
4. Have you examined your past fearlessly?
5. Did you admit the truth?

Have you completed these steps to the best of your ability? If you feel your work in the first five steps is solid, congratulations and please continue to Step 6.

Step 6 - Identify Your Deficiencies

During Step 5 you should have been able to identify certain deficiencies in perspective that repeatedly caused problems in your past. These would be any patterns you found during the self-examination work and going through it with God and another. The self-seeking behaviors that you default to during fearful situations or when you feel powerless are a big clue to your deficiencies. Finding these deficiencies and knowing they exist is the first step to allowing God to correct your perception during your day and allow him to manage them. This world makes us all a little crazy. A very important piece of us is missing that we need to make sense of this world. That piece is God. Without Him, we are lost. We are deficient and God is sufficient. That's the only way I can explain it.

When we ask him to remove our deficiencies in the next step, we are really asking him to help us rely on his sufficiency. The reason we have to ask him everyday, is because we are like the girl in 50 first dates who goes to bed and in the morning wakes up with no memory and has to look at a video to remember who she is. We need to remember each day to ask for His sufficiency so we don't forget and default to unconscious ego-driven behavior during our day. Here is an example of some of my deficiencies that I uncovered during my review of my 4th step work:

- Feel the need to be in control of everything
- Feeling sorry for myself
- Feeling fearful
- Never happy where I am
- Procrastinating
- Doubting myself
- Judging others
- Not setting boundaries
- People-pleasing
- Feeling shame
- Always thinking about myself
- Having to be the best at something
- Manipulating to get what I want
- Building grudges
- Impatience

Make a list of your deficiencies. For each of these deficiencies, we will be asking God in Step 7 to remove them. You need to be intimately familiar with them, because the circumstances which trigger your deficiencies will demand your attention and it is up to you to remember who is in control going forward and seek His help when you feel tempted to revert to unconscious behavior. Most of these deficiencies are ego-driven, and the circumstances which trigger them are the ego trying to put his foot in the door before it closes. We will create a cheat sheet of ways our manager can help us with them, so the ego can never use them against us again. These strategies I discovered from doing my 5th step with God and my sponsor and thinking about how self-reliance has failed me in the past when I was combating fear and powerlessness. Make a list of strategies you can employ to immediately get help from above when you are feeling insufficient. God can help you determine what these should be so pull up a chair for him. Here is an example using my deficits and how I will seek God's help if and when they appear:

- **Need to be in control of everything** - Realize most things that happen here are out of my control. I can't fix these things. God is in control! Thank God. Most of the things that happen here are none of my business. Let Go, and, Let God or God's will be done. Remember to enjoy the ride. Ask God to take care of things and trust that he is working everything out to my ultimate advantage. Realize I can hit the pause button and ask for God's intervention in a crisis situation, when I feel powerless and ask for an intuitive thought from above if I feel I must do something. If I feel I am crossing the line and trying to control another person's outcomes, tell them the way I handle

Danielle C. Pace

situations like this is to ask God for help, then direct them to do the same.

- **Feeling sorry for myself** - Realize I can't change the past. Know that everything happened for a reason and that I should use my past experience to help others. Would I allow one of my friends to lie around crying about the past? No, I would help them take their mind off the past. Shouldn't I care enough about myself to let God do the same for me? Forgive the past and ask God to help me get back to now. I watch the Melanie Martinez video version of "*It's my Party*" called "*Pity Party*" on youtube. It helps me to laugh at myself. Realize how utterly useless this emotion is and that because it is so negative, it can attract more negativity. This realization helps me to turn my life back to God and to more positive territory quickly. Using the "Phone a friend" lifeline is also a good way to get over feeling sorry for myself!

- **Feeling fearful** - "These fears are termites that ceaselessly devour the foundations of whatever sort of life we try to build" Alcoholics Anonymous 12 and 12, *Step Four*, p. 49. **Hit the pause button.** Ask God for a positive action I can take. Fear is **not real**, work through it with God's help. Immediately say "No defenses shall be made" this is an affirmation that making defenses will give my ego permission to take over and imagine all sorts of negative outcomes that it must guard against. This is no longer allowed! Ask God to remove the fear. Think of a silver lining outcome that could take place and picture it, feel it and be grateful for it. Be grateful and faithful not fearful. Ask God to put someone in my life who needs my help. This will take my mind off of my fears and any ineffectual defenses my ego might think up to make them seem real.

- **Never happy where I am** - To combat this, I should thank God for everyone in my life and everything I have. If I'm having trouble with that, get out a notebook and write 10 things I am grateful for. Use a trick from "The Magic" by Rhonda Byrne: Pick a gratitude rock and keep it by my bedside. Each night hold the rock and say the thing I am the most grateful for that day. Help someone less fortunate than myself. Pray that God remove my ungratefulness.

- **Procrastinating** - or "2 trash cans make a dumpster!" - heard in an AA meeting. Ask God what I should be doing instead. Don't let my todo's accumulate, do them. When I get behind, I can do the next thing on the list until I'm back on top of it. Realize the world won't collapse if I get behind and ask God to remove the fear that is keeping me from moving forward.

- **Doubting myself** - "A journey of a thousand miles begins with a single step" - Chinese proverb. Retrain myself to see that **nothing is impossible for God**. Realize that failure is a big part of success and don't be afraid of it. Every failure is a lesson learned. Every failure is another step closer to success. All of these small steps accumulate into one big success. I don't have to be perfect, God made me to be just perfectly me! Thank God that I can just be the best me I can be today. Ask God to help me see the journey for what it truly is and get on my way.

- **Judging others** - "You spot it you got it" - an AA favorite line. If I'm accusing someone else of something, maybe I am guilty of the same. Ask God to help me overcome the need to judge others. Don't participate when others are passing judgment on someone, this is the opposite of love. If I am judging someone else, I probably have found something I don't like about myself. Examine what fearful thought is causing me to judge someone else and ask God to help me overcome it. If I don't like being judged, why am I judging others. This is classic ego-driven behavior. Ask God to remove my need for judgment so I can know peace.

- **Not setting boundaries** - "Carry the message… not the mess" - heard in an AA meeting. Set positive boundaries with God's help, stay away from negativity. Don't build grudges. Speak my truth and don't be a silent witness. There is a fine line between helping others and doing for them what is not mine to do. Ask God to help me be a teacher and a leader, not an enabler. If I can, teach them what I know, otherwise stay out of their dramatic situations and tell them to seek God's help. Not everyone will get that their problems are between them and God. Don't get dragged into it. Negativity will crop up if I cross the line and try to control others or let them control me. Remember **who** is in control and ask God to help me walk away.

- **People-pleasing** - "Be yourself; everyone else is already taken." - Oscar Wilde. My life is my own to live, so be myself. Others opinions of me are not my concern. Picture someone disagreeing with me and being okay with it. Know that I can't please everyone - there are just too many opinions out there. Ask God to remind me that I don't have to argue my opinions. I can just say "We have differing opinions." Changing others opinions is not easy and not necessary. God would not want me to argue with anyone over an opinion, but to let it go. Let other people have their opinions - it is a better world when we aren't all exactly alike. Ask God to help me state my opinions in a kind manner and ask him to make me willing to humbly listen to others opinions. Be loving and kind to all, not just those who agree with me. Ask for God's serenity when someone is disagreeing with me and help me to be grateful for the person's good qualities and the fact that they feel strongly about something, whether I agree or not.

- **Feeling shame** - "Shame is the lie someone told you about yourself." - Anais Nin. Ask God to help erase shame from my life. Ask him to help me live my truth. Think of something I can do to serve others. Remember God doesn't want me being a judge and that means judging myself as well as others. Get out of the self appraisal business. Learn to laugh at myself more. Some of these things if they happened to someone else would be really funny. God has a sense of humor so he is probably laughing out load along with me. And remember God loves me anyways and he needs the unique me, with all my quirkiness. Stop taking myself so seriously.

- **Always thinking about myself** - "I'm not much but I'm all I think about" - Heard in an AA meeting. Put God first, and serve others. The rest will fall into place. Once I start helping others and sensing my purpose, I am released from the bondage of self. Self will has led me down a path of destruction and always thinking about selfish things was forefront on that path. Fulfilling my purpose to others is actually self-fulfillment at it's best. It makes me feel good to help others. If I find myself only thinking about myself, start the day over with the 3rd Step Prayer and ask God to put someone who needs my help in my path today.

- **Having to be the best at something** - There are many people in this world. I cannot be the best at everything. Stop comparing myself to others. I need to dial it back and just be me. Ask God to help me be willing to admit I am not the best at something and try to learn from those who are better at it, instead of judging them and trying to find fault. Be happy when I meet someone better at something than I am. This person could be a mentor to me in this area! How can I be the best me if I don't have mentors? Ask God to put mentors in my path and to help me recognize them. If I do have talent in a particular area, ask God to put people in my path that I can mentor.

- **Manipulating to get what I want** - Ask God to help me recognize when I am trying to manipulate others to get what I want. Ask him to help me be a lady of dignity and insight. Using flirting, guilt or blackmail are forms of attack. If I want something simply ask. It will either be given or not. No need to manipulate. Ask God to remind me of this when it is happening so I can focus on what is truly important, growing in knowledge and spirituality!

- **Building grudges** - "Grudge not, lest ye be grudged" – my take on Judge quote. Do I want others to bundle up all of my shortcomings into one big pile and not be able to get past them? No. That's what I am doing when I build a grudge. I will not allow my ego to take offense and create bad intentions for others. I will ask God to help me choose to forgive others shortcomings and learn to think the best of others. I will choose to see them from God's perspective and realize that they are humans and subject to ego the same as I.

- **Impatience** - "One minute of patience, ten years of peace." – Greek proverb. Get in the back seat metaphorically. God is in charge. Enjoy the ride. When someone cuts me off on the road, I can hit pause and count to ten. Forgiveness is Bliss! The car is a great place to practice patience, tolerance and forgiveness. Treat the drive as a luxury. A journey to be enjoyed in and of itself. Change my perspective: if I went back in time even 100 years ago, I wouldn't be able to get anywhere as quickly as I do now and in such style. The car is a magic machine! I should thank God everyday for the magical time in which I get to live.

Once you have listed your deficiencies, try to remember that they are rooted in fear of the past and insecurity for the future. The only place you can completely heal your past pain is by relinquishing it in the present. If you choose to relive past pain in the present, you are choosing to remain unconscious of your power to change. You are choosing to project the past into your present and you will not be able to evolve past the pain. Your future follows from the present so every present moment counts. Don't bring past pain into your present. You have the power to wipe all past pain off the map in your present. Every present moment when you choose joy and deny morbid reflection, deny knee-jerk reactions, deny ego it's ability to make fear seem real, is an affirmation that the past has lost it's power and your future is bright, joyous and peaceful. The ego will fight this because it thinks your identity is tied up with past pain and shouts for you to repeat it. It is not easy to ignore the shouting ego and many lessons will come when you begin to sense your power of ego-denial. Continue to strive for independence from knee-jerk ego reactions to feelings of inadequacy, guilt, fear, powerlessness, impatience etc., and you will find your peace in choice. The pause button is invaluable here. Pause and make a choice that you will not allow your ego to dominate your reaction to this test. Do a quick consult to remember who is in control. The ego will shout for you to control this new fearful situation the ego has projected from your past. It will shout for you to make defenses. What will your choice be? As the ego slowly loses it's power to project fear into your present, you will sense a new freedom and it will become easier to stay positive and recognize a call for love from one of your brothers. Everyone here is dealing with the same unconscious knee-jerk ego reactions to fear and it makes us all a little crazy. We lose our ability to ask for love in a sane manner and turn, quite unconsciously, to acting up. All the self-seeking behaviors you put down in step 4, turn-around question 3 were your cries for love and not pain in a situation where you felt fear and powerlessness. Hard to believe, but true. Now you are learning to recognize a call for love in a brother/sister and be able to see it as a response to his/her fears and respond appropriately not unconsciously. That is the power of awakening to God's plan and the relinquishment of your ego's plan. Ask God how you can make a conscious response to any fears projected towards you. Make no defenses because fear is not real. As it says in *"A Course in Miracles"* - "Nothing real can be threatened. Nothing unreal exists. Herein lies the peace of God."

Once you have listed all of your deficiencies and have a strategy to let God help you manage and eliminate them in the present, you should ask yourself if you are now entirely willing to give these self-serving, ego-centric deficits to God for management. **This is an important step because it means you will no longer default to ego-driven behavior and it is a commitment to God that you will consciously seek His help whenever these crop up. Here we ask God to help us be willing.**

Go to a place where you can be at peace for an hour, at least, before you make this important decision. Allowing Him to take management of your life means giving all predicaments to him for them to be removed from your ego's control. You will no longer be alone and entangled with your maniacal Captain Ahab. You will be joining with God, and with your brothers and sisters in faith in the future. The 7th Step is where you will be attesting to this commitment, but first you need to have your list and understand how you will give these to him and stop relying on self in the future. Carefully reread your list to determine your willingness to let each deficiency be managed by God and not your ego. How will you seek his help when you need it? This is a leap of faith and you are saying you will not go back to your island and unconsciously rely on your ego self. Are you now willing to ask him for help when each of these deficits surface and your ego tries to take over? When you are willing that all of your deficiencies be given to God for management, continue to Step 7.

Step 7 – Ask God to Remove Them

The 7th step prayer below is a specific prayer to ask God to remove our deficiencies each day and to give us strength to tackle issues with grace and faith so we may enjoy the flow of peace into our lives.

> *God, I am willing to submit my deficiencies to you during the day ahead. Please remove any selfish motives that would destroy my peace today. Please keep me from making defenses and direct my attention to who you would have me be. Grant me your strength to remove regret and worry from my day and replace these with serenity and faith.*

We have now completed Step 7. We are no longer an island unto ourselves. We have rejoined the shore as a part of the whole. Rejoice and let God strengthen you, guide you and lead the way each day. In the future, if you get blocked during your day, you can recite this 7th step prayer as a re-commitment of your promise to let him direct your steps and keep you on track today. Add this 7th step prayer to your Daily Prescription reading.

By the way, as you are now more than halfway through, you should sense a new energy and a new peace has come into your life. Are any of the Daily Prescription Promises beginning to come true? Has your outlook changed?

We are now ready to face our past and release ourselves from the chains that have kept us imprisoned and doomed to repeat its mistakes. We are ready to move to Step 8, but first a word about fellowship.

About Fellowship

In AA the fellowship is a big part of recovery. This is where you meet people who can help you stay sober and where you can provide service so that you stay out of self. Even if you are not in recovery from alcoholism, you are in recovery of not knowing and loving yourself, or of some other self-harming addiction. We all have some form of self-seeking behavior our ego uses to control us. For you to battle the ego, you need a fellowship around you that can help take your mind off your old idea of self long enough for you to build a new one. Believe me nothing can take your mind off your problems more than seeing someone else struggling and being able to lend them a helping hand. Sometimes just hearing your advice to someone else makes you realize what you are trying to tell yourself. Also, hearing others issues and how they are dealing with them makes you realize you aren't the only one with problems. If you are feeling really low, the worst thing you can do is to isolate and reminisce on all your past problems. This is like placing a call to the universe and asking for more problems. After you pray to God to remove your self pity, call someone and let them know you are struggling. More than likely they will have some good advice of something you can try or if not just knowing they are there for you can give you the feeling of bonding and fellowship that helps you through this difficult time. Any positive step is a step in the right direction.

The Greek myth *"King Midas and the Golden Touch"* tells of a king who wished that everything he touched would turn to gold. After getting his wish, he was surrounded by gold and was a very rich man. But was he? He realized when he touched his beloved daughter and she turned into a golden statue that real riches are not made of gold. This is a tale about not being bound by our own selfish desires. It took getting everything he thought he desired (materially) to appreciate what he already had (humanitarily). Is being rich monetarily ever going to really satisfy anyone? A truly rich man is one who has grown beyond the fantasy of wealth to the reality of love for others. It is in being with and helping others that a life of true riches will be found. That is the true everlasting gold. Do not wait until you are on your deathbed to realize this! I heard a funny line in a movie that you never see a hearse followed by a U-Haul. The Egyptians tried to take it with them and all they ever got was robbed! The only everlasting dents we will have on this world are the ones we leave on each others' hearts. Leave some good dents!

If you have a fellowship of people around you who know you and love you for who you are, then you are truly a rich man. To get to this, you first need to love yourself boldly and radically. If you don't truly love yourself, then how will you allow anyone else to love you? You are a unique and beautiful person. One of a kind. Set yourself in front of a mirror and speak affirmations. Look yourself in the eye and tell yourself that it is okay to start down a new path of self love. Tell yourself you are loved and you are beautiful. Reject any old ideas that were handed to you in the past. You are a brand new person everyday. You have the power to break old agreements you had with yourself and others. If you have people around you who criticize you, release that agreement. Start giving and accepting love first with yourself and then with everyone around you, and the agreements you have will change accordingly. You are the first member of your fellowship. Love yourself first, then the rest will come easily.

Begin to build your fellowship if you do not already have one. It can be comprised of people in your family, at work, in your community, in your place of worship. Your new manager will begin to put positive, like-minded people into your path, as well as those that need your help. Some will be mentors for you and some you will mentor. Grow this fellowship by sharing of yourself, your time and your talents. Even if you are just having a conversation with another person, this is fellowshipping. If you don't have many people to fellowship with, join a group on meetup.com, take an art class or join a club. It may feel awkward at first, but push through. God will help you find your fit. I actually have two fellowships in AA as I have moved but am still close to members of my original home group and I have a group of ladies at my worship center to fellowship with as well. These groups also will provide you with a chance to serve. When you start serving others, even if it's just to make them a cup of coffee, offer a ride to a meeting, or talk them through a tough time, you will begin to feel that your life has a purpose. You will want to be of more service. God wants to use you to help others. You have a unique talent to help others. It is important to find people you can help and hone your skills. He will let you know where your talents are needed. The more you help, the more you will want to help. We all want to feel we are needed.

You may not understand at first what you can do to help others. This is where your new manager will start showing you your purpose and talents you didn't realize you have. If you look up *purpose* on google, the definition is "the reason for which something is done or created or for which something exists." I was always looking for the reason I am here. I guess I was looking for my purpose, but looking in all the wrong places. So why am I here? What is my purpose for existing? It seems to be a moving target that I am discovering by using my talents to serve others. If I continue to follow orders from above, I don't really need to ask, because my purpose is evolving everyday. I can't wait each day to see what my purpose is today. As soon as I hit my knees and do my 3rd step prayer, I feel like God begins telling me his will for me today. I will get nudges or feelings that I should call someone. Today my job is to continue writing this book! I love reading and I've always loved writing so maybe that's why my manager gave me this assignment. If there is another assignment, I will get a call or something will happen while I'm doing this today. When I'm paying attention and doing the next right thing, the next job for me will appear. So I will keep writing until then.

Weirdly everything that used to be on my calendar, including my job, disappeared for awhile so I could devote time to writing this book. I had been working full-time, so even though losing my job was hard, it seems to have been a part of my purpose and God's will for me. I think the opportunity to write a book which may help others, with my manager's help of course, may be the reason my schedule was cleared. Who knows. Weirder things have happened lately, like a much better job, so I don't rule it out. Knowing God is in charge helps me to realize I will be okay no matter the present circumstances I find myself in.

Your new manager is also in your fellowship. If it's the middle of the night and your mind is rehashing something that happened 20 years ago, you can ask him to help you get back to sleep. He usually tells me to read a book and that puts me back to sleep pretty quickly. He's available always and he has all the answers so if you ask he will find a way to get you the answer. Once you start realizing that coincidences are not coincidental, you will know he is out there trying to tell you something. Einstein once said "coincidence is God's way of remaining Anonymous". God always answers though sometimes we don't realize it.

As you fellowship with others, you will start to recognize clues in something they say to you. God speaks through others and often is trying to give you a hint about something he wants you to pursue. He even talks through shows on TV, songs on the radio and words you read. Animals and plants can be a part of your fellowship too. If the birds are particularly squawky I know he's trying to tell me something. Pets are definitely part of your fellowship. They are great listeners and can send you good vibes. Make sure you are open to receiving His messages. Spend more time listening than talking. An acronym we have in AA is WAIT which is "Why Am I Talking?" Through your fellowship with others, you will get new assignments and learn of things you can do to be of service, so always listen carefully and build your fellowship.

As you begin to recognize His form of communication to you, remember that His communications are always positive and loving. The point is to always see everything in a loving light. Even though something could be interpreted negatively, you must choose to interpret it with love. This will always be the correct interpretation, is what I have learned. He stressed this continually to me until I memorized it. Love reinforces love and love casts out fear. Fear is your ego misinterpreting. Don't misinterpret God. Interpreting positively invokes faith, interpreting negatively invokes fear. So, if you see a sign and it makes you fearful, change your perception. That is why the more positivity you choose to see, the more positive your life will become. So always choose to see everything in a positive light. No matter if everyone calls you PollyAnna, you are correct and that is all there is to it.

There is a great little book titled "Zen And the Art of Happiness" by Chris Prentiss that helped me understand the power of a positive mindset in all things. It is a short, but very important read. Chris' message is that everything that happens to you is for your good and even when it seems bad, you must push through it and have the attitude that some good will come even in the midst of tragedy. This is the positive message God would like you to see behind the scenes of any addiction recovery program. Addictions can be **cured by a spiritual connection**, and in the maintenance of that spiritual connection, need not ever return. Not only do we need to find our connection, but to maintain and grow it through fellowship, positivity and faith.

As you continue building your fellowship, be alert for clues that will help you realize your own perfect purpose unfolding. As you work the remaining steps, grow your faith and fellowship. You are ready for Step 8.

Step 8 – Make a List of Those You Have Wronged

Our resentments separate us from other people, God and from finding ourselves. The key that we were partly responsible for them is the reason we now need to learn to humbly accept our part in creating these resentments. Admitting our mistakes (making amends) to those we had resentments against cleans up our side of the street and allows us to finally release any anger or guilt over past mistakes. We are getting rid of any residual negativity the ego could use to manipulate us in the future. We are releasing the fears that our ego made us believe were real. As the Big Book says, "We attempt to sweep away the debris which has accumulated out of our effort to live on self-will and run the show ourselves." - *Big Book of Alcoholics Anonymous, Pg. 76*

First, we need to categorize each name in our notebook for the persons we had resentments against in the past. Here are the categories that you can put the names in.

1. Easily accessible (see them quite often and you are willing to make amends)
2. Close family and friends (easily accessible and you are willing to make amends)
3. Pray for Willingness (not quite ready but you will pray for willingness)
4. Don't think I should or not appropriate (would hurt others or dredge up more resentments)
5. Not easily accessible but willing (don't see them or have lost touch)
6. Living Amends (yourself, God, and anyone who has died or is inaccessible)

Categorizing your list of resentments will show you which ones you should make amends to. It acknowledges that you want to put the past in your rear view mirror. For the list you create, put the Category and then list each Person with the number from your original list so you can easily look them up and see what you are making amends for. Leave a couple of lines between each name so you can list your self-seeking behaviors. Cross out any that speaking about with the person might be hurtful to them. We are not trying to hurt someone. You don't have to go into specifics, either. If you have nothing to say that isn't hurtful, you can always say I could have been a better friend, brother, daughter, etc. We stick to our own faults not the other persons.

Once you have made your list, you are ready to begin making amends. Continue to Step 9.

Step 9 - Make amends

Take your list out and begin making amends. They can be done over the phone, however try to do them in person, if possible. They do not need to be done in any order, just as you see fit. For the living amends section, write a letter to the person. Making amends affirms your tie to others by your admission of your part in resentments. Forgiveness is the path to miracles as stated in "A Course in Miracles", so make sure you apply for all of your miracles.

You may want to listen to the guided meditation "God's Prescription for Forgiveness" before each amends you make. Being willing to look at your part in these resentments will help you to move forward positively in your current and future relationships. It is not easy to make these amends, but once you have, you will understand why it is important. The script for your amends can go something like this -

"Hi, this is John Doe can I have 5 minutes of your time. I am working a 12 step program where making amends where we've been wrong is important. I would like to make amends for xxx. " specify your actions or generalize ask them if there is anything you missed. Be willing to listen and validate if they have additional input. Towards the end of the conversation say something like "God willing, this will never happen again." and make sure to thank them for their time.

After each one, check them off your list. You don't have to complete all of them before continuing to step 10. Complete 4 or 5 and then continue. Do try to make all of your amends, as each one brings new freedom to your life.

Below are a list of promises that should be coming true for you now. Continue reading and reaching for them daily:

- You will learn what things really are your business and what is indeed out of your control.
- You will find freedom in releasing the need for control.
- This freedom will bring you a new-found purpose that will truly satisfy your desires for this life.
- You will lose interest in living in the past or trying to re-arrange the future and find meaning and joy in the ever-evolving present.

- Peace will overcome fear and self-pity will disappear.
- You will have a new manager to guide you and you will find that God is the driving force behind your new design for living.
- You will begin living a life that is happy, joyous and free.

Step 10 – Continue to Review Daily

Step 10 is to continue to make a daily review and to set right any mistakes you make as you follow this new design for living. You are meant to feel happy, joyous and free and this is not possible if you are carrying around guilt, worry or resentments. Break your old routines. Break old agreements. Start your day joyously, gratefully. Everyday is a new day to be amazed with your new design for living. Every evening, review your day and take account of what you got right and what you got wrong. The reason for this accounting is to get rid of everything that isn't working and replace it with new habits. This daily reflection is a testament and a promise to continue seeking love of yourself and others everyday. How can you change your perception if you don't evaluate your day and make amends quickly when you have been wrong. This is the way to change from selfish ego-driven, unsatisfying lives to free, joyous and meaningful ones. This is how to find your true purpose. Extend this new design for living into all you do. With this daily tenth step, you can enrich your spiritual life so your ego cannot gain back ground. In AA we say your ego is doing push-ups in the background just waiting for it's chance to regain control. A daily tenth step will shine the light on ego ploys, and keep you honest.

Continue your daily reading of **Chapter 7. Daily Prescription** as this reminds you daily how you have committed to seek God in prayer and meditation and evaluate your daily performance. You will find many times during the day when you can use prayer and meditation to reach out for intuitive thought and will soon find that you rely on God in all dilemmas. When you are not happy, joyous and free, you should now feel that something is not right and you now know to seek God at these times. Ask God to remove the fears that are once again invading your peace and at once turn your attention to what he would have you **be**. He wants you to **be free** of these fears and feel joy and peace. Give all fears to God. You cannot conquer something that isn't real, and you cannot allow your ego to make defenses. Continue to grow your spiritual condition by asking for God's will daily. In this step, we promise to keep our routine from becoming routine. Evaluate what is working and what is not. Grow your spiritual muscles by reaching out in faith for answers each day. If you are sliding back into ego, it is most assuredly because your routine is not working.

You now have a new Manager and you should be consulting with him everyday. By doing so, you will begin to sense his strength supporting you. Relying on him during a crisis is what he expects. If you had issues during the day that you could have given to Him and you didn't, make sure to give them to him at the end of the day. He wants to help you and to steer you in the right direction, but he needs your trust to do so. You no longer have to solve everything for everyone and you don't have to play God. Become as trusting as a child and know that you are loved and you have a protector. Fear should begin to leave you and you will begin to sense that all fear is unreal and demands a perspective shift. When you find yourself having to stifle laughter when someone else tells you their fears, you will know you are finally getting it. Give all fear and worry to God and just BE. BE happy, BE joyous and BE free.

Continue to Step 11.

Step 11 - Seek God thru Prayer & Meditation

Now that we have made conscious contact with God, how can we maintain and even enhance our relationship? We must continue to grow in faith and for this, we can utilize prayer and meditation. Anytime we ask God for His help, we are praying. Anytime we listen to God's response, we are meditating. So this step is all about communication with our New Manager. God expects us to ask for and receive inspiration and direction during our day and as we do this, we begin to grow in Spirit. We begin to understand why it is in our best interest to ask God because he can see the big picture and we cannot. We soon realize that meditating and waiting to hear God's answer allows our will to align with His will for us and frees us from kneejerk reactions and from responding out of fear. I once heard someone in a meeting say "If you only pray, you will never get any answers, praying without meditating is like calling God on the phone, telling him all of your problems and then hanging up when he starts to answer." Don't hang up on God! We need to build our spiritual muscles with regular prayer and meditation. There are prayers in Appendix I that may help you when you are facing issues which require a guided approach to prayer. There are also guided meditations in audio format which were designed for this book for you to try if you don't have any meditations you are already using. There are many books on meditation at the library as well if you want to learn more about various forms and techniques.

The prayers in Appendix I were created by my dear and lovely friend Julie F. who has stood by me during my AA adventure. She created them to go with my God's Pharmacy meditations. She has provided them as stand-alone prayers for each virtue or as one longer prayer to ask God for all virtues. I hope her lovely words will inspire you in your devotions.

The guided meditations I created to go along with this book are designed to help you relax and empower you to be in tune with God throughout the day. The premise for these meditations is that you are praying to God in the morning to ask for a particular virtue that you might need to work on during your day. The meditation for that topic is meant to help you realize you can reach out to God at anytime you need Him during your day for help. We all need guidance from God each day and these meditations aim to help you reach Him. During the meditations you will take a trip to God's pharmacy to fill a prescription only God can fill. Listen to the guided meditation *God's prescription for...* whichever virtue you have prayed for. Each of the 7 approximately seven-minute meditations has a central theme. The topics are Love, Gratitude, Perception, Wisdom, Patience, Forgiveness and Faith. For instance, during your morning prayer, you might ask God for His help with forgiveness or gratitude today. Afterwards, find a quiet place to listen to the relevant guided meditations. You will be entering God's pharmacy and finding essential items that God has infused during your meditation to give you His strength during your day. These prescriptions may help you be mindful of others you encounter today with wisdom, patience and love or help you change your perception through joy, grace, forgiveness and faith. All scripts for the guided meditations can be found in Appendix II and the audio versions can be found on my youtube channel by opening youtube and searching for "Danielle C. Pace". Make sure you also save some quiet time for traditional meditation during the day so you can hear directly from God.

Try to find a quiet place where you can pray and meditate and print out some prayers to place there. I have a spiritual corner setup in my bedroom where I keep my spiritual books, prayers and my headphones for listening to guided meditations. I have printed the "Peace Prayer" or "Prayer of Saint Francis" and the prayers from Appendix I so they are easily available when I need them.

The Prayer of Saint Francis

Lord, make me an instrument of your peace
Where there is hatred, let me sow love
Where there is injury, pardon
Where there is doubt, faith
Where there is despair, hope
Where there is darkness, light
And where there is sadness, joy

O Divine Master, grant that I may
Not so much seek to be consoled as to console
To be understood, as to understand
To be loved, as to love

For it is in giving that we receive
And it's in pardoning that we are pardoned
And it's in dying that we are born to Eternal
Life
Amen.

Step 12 - Carry the Message to Others

It would be nice if everyone had a program where they would think before acting and try to make kinder, more loving decisions. The twelfth step asks that if you have followed instructions, let God hire you, and found this new design for living to have changed you, to kindly pass it on to others. If you find someone struggling, your experience could give them hope that they desperately need. Many people here are struggling and they may not understand that a spiritual solution is available to them. When they hear you have found an answer which involves God, they may shy away or not believe you, but a seed is planted. They will certainly be attracted to the peaceful energy you are emitting. They may see you happy, joyous and free and wonder how they can get what you have. They may start on a wonderful journey of discovery just from the truth of your words and your presence. Tell them what has helped you and that God is available if they wish to make contact. Tell them about your spiritual awakening. If they are open to it, or become open to it, tell them what you know of God. We are all witnesses of what we choose to see. Of what we choose to believe. If you had addictions or resentments that were destroying your life that you have overcome using these steps, you could be just the person to help others with the same problems you had. Your experience is a testimony that can uniquely speak to them.

That is all that is asked in this final step. God has hired you to use your talents to reach others, and to find your unique purpose. Be open to those that God sends to you. We are all connected so if one of us is suffering, we all are. The sooner we come to this conclusion, the better for all of mankind. Help one another by spreading God's message of love so we can make a more peaceful world for ourselves, our children, our nations, our world, our universe. Nothing is more important although it may seem to be. God has given us free will to decide what path we will follow. He hopes that you will choose His path for you, which means leaving your small island of you to join Him in reaching out to his other children.

Entangled Forever

Becoming entangled with the Great Spirit of the Universe changed the course of my life. I am grateful that my desperate cry for help at what I thought was the bitter end is where my life with His Grace began. The 12 step program He brought me to, and the fellowship that surrounded me there helped me find this relationship with God and to finally love myself. Words can never express my gratefulness for this gift. The only way I can even come close is to pay it forward, spread the message and help others become entangled with God, as I am. When I see someone suffering I always tell them how much God loves them and how unique they are. That is God's work. He wants us to spread knowledge of His love for us and that we should love ourselves and each other as He does.

Being entangled with God's energy, is to me, a form of quantum entanglement. What does that mean? *"Quantum entanglement is a mechanical phenomenon in which the quantum states of two or more objects have to be described with reference to each other, even though the individual objects may be spatially separated. This leads to correlations between observable physical properties of the systems."* In other words the systems no longer operate separately or individually. Now that I am entangled, I cannot continue to believe that I live separately. My lines are tangled together with God's. Kind of like the Borg in Star Trek or the Force in Star Wars, it is a tether that connects us. That is how I see this sixth sense of entanglement with the Great Spirit of the Universe operating. Once we connect to God, the sixth sense tethers us to Him and through Him to all of His creation.

So, like the famous lines from Melville in Moby Dick, "Thou canst never return", once you know God and His love for you, you become entangled. You can never return to your island where you will be all alone. You are never truly alone again. Once you truly know God, your lines are entangled with His and when he moves, you move and vice-versa! Unlike Ahab you need no longer be ruled by your maniacal ego, or a puppet to fear. Like Ishmael you have escaped this fate through faith. It is these lines from Moby Dick which lead me to believe that Ishmael, the narrator and sole survivor of Ahab's crew, was possessed of a certain faith:

> *"...And some certain significance lurks in all things, else all things are little worth, and the round world itself but an empty cipher,*

except to sell by the cartload, as they do the hills about Boston, to fill up some morass in the Milky Way." - Herman Melville "Moby Dick", CHAPTER 99, The Doubloon. Paragraph 2

"But even so, amid the tornadoed Atlantic of my being, do I myself still for ever centrally disport in mute calm; and while ponderous planets of unwaning woe revolve around me, deep down and deep inland there I still bathe me in eternal mildness of joy."- Herman Melville "Moby Dick", CHAPTER 87, The Grand Armada. Paragraph 28

Ishmael found his way to eternal joy. Your ego would like to isolate you and keep you on an island, shackled hopelessly to fear and bitter resentment. Set on a wayward course, in a relentless search for peace, just out of reach, in some distant future. God wants you to reach out in faith and love and become entangled with Him, and realize that His peace surrounds you in the here and now. Forever available in this present moment. This present moment can then extend to eternity. In the end it is your choice, but I hope you get your lines irreversibly entangled with God's, and become a testament to the term "happy, joyous and free."

Appendix I - Prayers

Love

God, I love you and need you in my life today. I ask that you fill my heart with your radiant love throughout this day, so that I may be the light of Your love for others. Please keep my heart overflowing, so that the power of your love shines through in every word I say and every step I take this day. Fill me with Your love so that I may be love.

Gratitude

God, I love you and I need you in my life today. I ask that you fill my heart with Your grace and mercy. Please help me to share my gratitude for your grace in every step I take and every word that escapes my lips today. Please help me to be thankful for every blessing you put in my day that comes by the way of people you put in my life, my family, friends and home. Thankfully yours...

Perception

God, I love you and I need you in my life today. Please fill my heart with joy and wonder. Please help my eyes to see the world through the lens of your love and carefree vision. Please allow your joy and wonder to flow through my being throughout this day and align my heart and actions with your vision.

Wisdom

God, I love you and need you in my life today. Please fill my heart with knowledge of your will. Please help me to understand your will and apply it in my life throughout this day. I ask that you keep me calm when I am unsure and put me in the direction you would have me go.

Patience

God, I love you and I need you in my life today. Please remove any impatience that may catch me off guard and help me to pause if anxiety or anger creeps into my heart. Please keep me in faith and help me be aware of the angels you put in my life throughout this day.

Forgiveness

God, I love you and I need you in my life today. I need your help forgiving _____.

Please help me to love this person as you do and create the miracle of forgiveness in my life.

Faith

God, I love you and I need you in my life today. Please help me to trust and rely on you when my faith is being tested. Please help my faith grow and open my heart to the challenges I may face today.

Prayer for All Virtues

God, I love you and need you in my life today. I ask that you fill my heart with your radiant love throughout this day, so that I may be the light of Your love for others. Please keep my heart overflowing, so that the power of your love shines through in every word I say and every action I take this day. Please help me to share my gratitude for your grace in every step I take and every word that escapes my lips today. Please help my eyes to see the world through the lens of your love and carefree vision, and allow your joy and wonder to flow through me. Please help me to understand your will and apply it in my life. I ask that you keep me calm when I am unsure and put me in the direction you would have me go. Please remove any impatience that may catch me off guard and help me to pause if anxiety or anger creeps into my heart. I ask that you help create the miracle of forgiveness in my life. Please help my faith grow and open my heart to the challenges I may face today.

Appendix II – Guided Meditations

Guided Meditations - God's Pharmacy:

God's Prescription for Love

Relax and breathe deeply... Let your mind clear of all thoughts...
Today realize you are not alone...
The Great Spirit of the Universe is here with you...
Ask for and receive his help today... God wishes for you to be filled with love today...
He has given you an unlimited refill of love...
You may return as often as you like...
See yourself in front of a magnificent building...
This is God's Pharmacy...
Enter in and pause...
You are in a large round Lobby with marble floors and a brightly lit foyer with dark blue seating...

There are 7 more doors arranged around the center of the lobby…
From the left, the doors are Love, Gratitude, Perception, Wisdom, Patience, Forgiveness and Faith
There is a display shelf to your left with many shopping bags of varied colors and patterns to choose from…
Select your favorite to put your prescription in…
Breathe deeply and relax…
To fill your prescription for love, Proceed to the door on your far left…
the door is Painted Red and has the word LOVE written in Gold on it…
The handle is in the shape of an arrow pointing inside…
as you open the door you feel a wave of love rushing over you…
Enter in, pause and take a deep breath…
You have entered an Atrium… within is a park-like setting.
breathe in the scent of roses and hear the lovely birds chirping…
A stone path leads down beside a lively flowing creek…
walk down the path to the creek…
Listen to the cascading water as the spring fed creek meanders around the Atrium and passes through several waterfalls…
The birds come to land nearby and chirp their hello…
The squirrels dart out, flick their tails and chatter in welcome…
Breathe deeply knowing you are loved in this place…
The Atrium air is moist and cool…

Pause to feel the crisp gentle breeze on your skin…
There is a step where you can sit next to the stream…
Sit and dangle your hand in the water a moment…
There are vibrant pink and red hearts filled with light
floating by in the creek,
reach down and select as many of these love lights as you
want…
Notice that you can pop them open to release God's
glorious love…
Pop open one of the hearts and love pours out in a
radiant light wave…
The glow ripples and spreads slowly illuminating
everything around you …
The air suddenly smells sweeter… A cotton candy like
smell…
Breathe in the sweet scent and relax…
Throughout your day, you will have more of these love
lights to pop open and spread love to others…
It will give you great joy to spread this love!
Take a deep breath and feel the love that is in this place…
Notice the wondrous trees in the Atrium …
They are filled with all different colors of heart-shaped
fruit…
The trees send you love and bend to offer you fruit…
Reach into the branches and pick as many heart fruit as
you want to place in your bag…
Sit down on the grass to relax…
Feel the sun beating down through the Atrium glass as it
gently kisses your skin…
Breathe in the liquid gold sunshine…

Choose one of the fruits and taste it…
There are no seeds and it is the perfect size…
This one is sweet and juicy and it tastes like a peach…
The skin melts in your mouth… it is as smooth as a grape's skin…
Enjoy the flavor and texture of the fruit and swallow it…
Breathe deeply, relax and let the love flow through your bloodstream, as it infuses you with warmth and delight…
You will be able to eat one of these heart fruits anytime during your day when you need to restock your love stores…
You will never run out of love… You have an unlimited prescription…
You are overflowing and wish to share this love…
Breathe deeply… Feel God's love surrounding you in this place…
Notice the beautifully colored butterflies as they flit by you…
They feel your love and tip their wings in return…
Stroll leisurely through the meadow to the otherside of the atrium
Notice the brightly-colored roses as they reach out to greet you…
Smell their sweet fragrance and feel their love…
In all you do today, reach out in love…
The exit back to the lobby appears before you…
Breathe deeply…
Use your love lights and heart fruit today to remember God is with you and his love surrounds you…
God's love for you is ever present and everlasting…

God's Prescription for Gratitude

Relax and breathe deeply... Let your mind clear of all
thoughts...
Today realize you are not alone...
The Great Spirit of the Universe is here in grace with
you...
Ask for and receive his grace today...
God wishes for you to be filled with gratitude today...
He has given you an unlimited refill of gratitude...
You may return as often as you like...
See yourself in front of a magnificent building...
This is God's Pharmacy...
Enter in and pause...
You are in a large round Lobby with marble floors
and a brightly lit foyer with dark blue seating...
There are 7 more doors arranged around the center of the
lobby...
From the left, the doors are Love, Gratitude, Perception,
Wisdom, Patience, Forgiveness and Faith
There is a table in the middle of the lobby with wooden
boxes, oblong in shape
The boxes have beautiful engravings carved into them
Choose your favorite box to hold your prescription...
Breathe deeply and relax...
To fill your prescription for gratitude, Proceed to the door
second from the left...
the door is a large gray stone arch door
the word GRATITUDE is beveled into it in Wizard
script...

there is a large brass knocker right beneath the lettering
the door is heavy, but as you push, it begins to move as if
by magic
as soon as you are in, the door closes behind you with an
echoed boom
take a deep breath and relax...
there is a rock walkway leading up to a gray stone castle
with round turrets...
The cool air hits you as you walk up the path past lush,
fragrant pine trees...
Breathe in the fresh pine scent...
When you get to the castle, you see large iron gates with a
Coat of Arms and the word Gratis below it
The name "Grace Castle" is emblazoned on the archway,
the gates magically open before you...
Walk through the gates into the hallway of the castle
There is a large picture wall... on the left
There are many frames but they are all empty...
As you pass each one, loved ones slide into the frames and
become animated...
A feeling of gratitude overcomes you, as you see yourself
having fun and reaching milestones...
You feel thankful as you relive some of these magic
moments...
Birthday parties, camping trips, shared smiles...
More frames and more pictures of friends, pets, loved
ones, good times you shared together...
some of the events seem to be in the future - people you
have yet to meet...
Ahead there's a table with magic wands...

Tap Into The Power Of God

A sign says "choose a wand and enter"
Choose your magic wand and enter the large foyer ahead
There is a ring with a star in the middle
proceed to the star, take a deep breath and raise the
wand…
When you wave the wand, God will show you more to be
grateful for…
With each wave of the wand, you paint your graces…
holographic images appear and form around you…
Special times you have had and will have seem to form
and then fade
you smile as they come and go…
A deep contentment fills you…
pets who have graced your life with their unconditional
love come to see you…
you send them love and thanks…
Take a deep breath and look around as more is revealed
to be grateful for…
your hologram graces dance and whirl around you…
they wave goodbye and scamper back into the wand
available when needed…
you will have it during your day to help you remember
this gratefulness…
When you are feeling ungrateful and stressed, take it out,
and let your symphony of gratitude play out around
you…
take a deep breath…
walk past the stone columns on the right and into an open
courtyard…
There is a large rock polisher in the middle, which is

noisily churning out rocks
The rocks tumble out and fall onto a conveyer belt…
At the end, they land in a large bin…
Go to the bin and pick out a very special rock…
It is smooth and round… This is a gratitude rock…
The instructions for it are:
Be counting your blessings during the day…
At the end of each day, hold this rock in your hand and
say the thing that you were most grateful for today…
Place your gratitude rock and magic wand in your
prescription box
Kneel down on one knee…
Breathe in and relax…
Thank God for his mercy and grace…
Feel His loving arms enveloping you in this place…
God's gratitude will go with you today infusing you with
gratefulness for all you have…
Miraculous things happen when you feel grateful…
The door to the lobby appears before you, stand up and
walk through it
As you close the door to Grace Castle, you are full of
God's grace…
Breathe Deeply….
Use your magic wand to count your blessings today and
take your gratitude rock from your box, at the end of the
day…
hold it close and say what you are most grateful for…
Thank God for His amazing grace…

God's Prescription for Perception

Relax and breathe deeply... Let your mind clear of all thoughts...
Today realize you are not alone...
The Great Spirit of the Universe is here to help you see the truth...
Ask for and receive his help today... God wishes for you to be filled with joy today...
He has given you an unlimited refill to help your perception today...
You may return as often as you like...
See yourself in front of a magnificent building...
This is God's Pharmacy...
Enter in and pause...
You are in a large round Lobby with marble floors and a brightly lit foyer with dark blue seating...
There are 7 more doors arranged around the center of the lobby...
From the left, the doors are Love, Gratitude, Perception, Wisdom, Patience, Forgiveness and Faith
There is a display shelf to your left with many shopping bags of varied colors and patterns to choose from...
Select your favorite bag to put your prescription in...
Breathe deeply and relax...
To fill your prescription for perception, proceed to the door third from the left...
the door is a large mirror and distorts your image as you draw close
the word PERCEPTION in holographic form is written

on it ...
PERCEPTION shifts to ARCADE when you get closer to it...
When you open the door... you feel excitement rush to greet you"'
Inside there are arcade games, numerous rides and a large fountain in the center...
The fountain has Orange liquid flowing out of it...
There are children running about laughing and having fun
Ah, Breathe in the energy of youth
a child rushes up eagerly and offers you some Orange drink from the fountain
she says it is Peter Pan Pop
you normally don't drink sweet drinks but you are thirsty...
the drink is so refreshing... you drink the whole cup...
after drinking it, you feel yourself getting smaller
You are slowly changing into a kid again!
You are regaining energy you thought was gone forever
You look down at your hands, they are those of a child...
you feel a surge of excitement, the wonder of this place suddenly dawns on you
you want to run and jump... laugh and play... You have so much energy...
Take a quick breath, you feel joy... you feel free...
All your adult cares have disappeared...
racing over to the playground you climb the slide all the way to the top
You feel so alive...

Tap Into The Power Of God

You feel the adrenalin rush as you slide down
You remember how much fun it is to run and play…
The other kids are rushing to the bumper cars
You run with them and find the perfect car… you are so
excited…
You jump in behind the wheel…
The music begins to play a disco beat…
you drive around bumping other kids cars and laughing…
Bumper cars are so much fun…
It is surprising how accepting and friendly the other
children are, even though you don't know them, and some
of them speak different languages…
You feel connected… you feel accepted…
The music stops, you exit and run with the other children
to the carousel
make your way up the ramp and choose a carousel horse
…
Jump up and feel the anticipation as the music begins to
play
The horses and the music start going faster, and then
faster,
you feel the wind whistling by, blowing through your
hair…
Listen to the laughter and music…
As you pass by the mirror you see yourself reflected as a
child…
You miss that smiling, laughing, carefree child…
God wants you to remember this feeling, this freedom…
Breathe in the excitement…
When you leave the carousel, the attendant gives all the

children their very own SpyGlass
He says you can see anything you want through the eyes
of a child with this special glass
Looking through your SpyGlass, you see the joy and
wonder of being young…
Everything looks more vibrant and lively and somehow
different
Joy surrounds and envelops you…
You can see and feel this wonder anytime during the day
by looking through your SpyGlass
Take a seat on the bench beside you…
Place your SpyGlass in your prescription bag…
Breathe in and relax…
You are slowly getting big again…
You rush over to the fountain,
grab a canteen, and fill it from the spigot to the brim with
the orange punch, and place it in your bag…
Anytime you want to feel like a kid again, joyous and
free,
you can open your canteen and drink some Pop to
remember this feeling…
You watch the kids for awhile as you slowly return to
adult-size…
Realize you are as young as you feel…
Allow yourself to feel this wonder, freedom, joy and unity
that children feel once again
The exit back to the lobby appears before you…
The archway says "See the world through different eyes"
As you close the door to the arcade, you know you can see
things more joyously today

Breathe Deeply…
Find time to be in the now today, not in the past or the
future, but completely present and in the moment…
God wants you to see through a different lens today…
Change your perspective…
Use your canteen of pop and SpyGlass throughout the
day to access joy and childlike wonder…
You always have access to His unlimited and never
ending joy…

God's Prescription for Wisdom

Relax and breathe deeply… Let your mind clear of all
thoughts…
Today realize you are not alone…
The Great Spirit of the Universe is here to guide you in
all your dilemmas…
Ask for and receive his guidance today… God wishes for
you to be filled with wisdom today…
He has given you an unlimited refill of wisdom…
You may return as often as you like…
See yourself in front of a magnificent building…
This is God's Pharmacy…
Enter in and pause…
You are in a large round Lobby with marble floors
and a brightly lit foyer with dark blue seating…
There are 7 more doors arranged around the center of the
lobby…
From the left, the doors are Love, Gratitude, Perception,
Wisdom, Patience, Forgiveness and Faith

*There is a display shelf to your left with many shopping
bags with different colors and patterns to choose from
Select your favorite bag to put your prescription in...
Breathe deeply and relax...
To fill your prescription for wisdom, proceed to the door
in the center...
the door is made of cherry wood and has the word
WISDOM engraved in polished brass...
As you open the door you see a vast array of books
Enter in and take a deep breath...
breathe in the scent of cherry wood and leather...
You are entering a large library...
There is a librarian station at the center ...
Several desks with plush leather chairs run in a row
down each side of the library...
Signs point to various subjects and interests...
A spiral staircase leads up to a mezzanine level with even
more stacks...
You are surrounded by rich cherry wood floors and walls,
and large wood beams frame the ceiling above you...
within this library is a treasure trove of wisdom on any
and all subjects...
God wants you to know Him and partake of His wisdom
and knowledge...
Make your way to the center near the librarians desk...
If you know what subject you are looking for, think of
that subject, and open your bag...
The correct books will fly from God's shelves and into
your bag...
Repeat until you have exhausted the subjects you wish to*

study today…
Ask the librarian to choose some books you will need for your day as well, and open your bag…
the librarian disappears and briefly reappears by each shelf as she collects your books…
She reappears in front of you and places the books you will need today in your bag…
You thank her and sit down at the desk on your left…
Relax into the soft leather chair…
you have everything you need…
you feel the calm and peace of this library…
reach into your prescription bag and randomly grab a book
open it… A wisp of smoke rises in curlicues and spirals from the spine, and then extends out around you…
Breathe deeply of the essence of wisdom…
Feel God's knowledge transferring to your subconscious…
This knowledge will be accessible when you need it today…
Simply ask a question and wait for the answer to be conveyed over to your conscious mind…
Any time you need wise counsel today,
open your bag, take out a book and open it to any page, read a few paragraphs…
then relax and wait for the cloud around you to infuse you with God's wisdom
The answer will come like a light bulb being turned on…
That's when you know it's from Him…
Sometimes it will just be an idea of where to find the answer or who can help you…

God gives us knowledge in many different ways… be open to any clues He gives…
Relax for a moment and feel the grace of not having to know all the answers…
You have access to God's vast store of knowledge anytime you need it…
Walk thru the library to the back coffee bar…
Sit down at the bar and smell the rich aroma of coffee brewing
Relax and breathe deeply
The barista comes around the side of the bar and offers you your pick from a large assortment of knowledge bite brownies
take as many brownies as you will need for the day…
Choose one of the brownies and eat it…
This one has a mint flavor and mint chips in it…
feel ideas swirling through the flavors in your mouth and straight to your mind…
sense God's wisdom coming to the surface and rippling into your consciousness…
anytime you are in doubt today, pause, relax and have a knowledge bite brownie
You will receive the perfect bit of wisdom straight from God's Coffee Bar…
breathe deeply…
He is with you and always has an answer to any predicament you find yourself in…
relax, eat a brownie and do a quick consult, the answer will come…
Take a stroll around the library and see the volumes of

books you have yet to check out…
As you exit, remember to thank God for this generous
unlimited library of knowledge
Use your books and knowledge bite brownies throughout
the day to access God's wisdom
You do not have to know all the answers, you have access
to His limitless library

God's Prescription for Patience

Relax and breathe deeply… Let your mind clear of all
thoughts…
Today realize you are not alone…
The Great Spirit of the Universe is here for you…
Ask for and receive his help today… God wishes for you
to be filled with serenity today…
He has given you an unlimited refill of patience…
You may return as often as you like…
See yourself in front of a magnificent building…
This is God's Pharmacy…
Enter in and pause…
You are in a large round Lobby with marble floors
and a brightly lit foyer with dark blue seating…
There are 7 more doors arranged around the center of the
lobby…
From the left, the doors are Love, Gratitude, Perception,
Wisdom, Patience, Forgiveness and Faith
There is a kiosk to your right with car keys hanging from
it…
Each set of keys has a label showing what year, make and

model the car keys are for...
Select a set of keys to your favorite car...
Breathe deeply and relax...
To fill your prescription for patience, proceed to the door
third from the right...
the door is chrome blue and has a car door handle to open
it
the word PATIENCE is written in chrome
and God's Motor Company Symbol is underneath...
push the OPEN button on your remote and the door
opens automatically...
as soon as you enter, you realize you are inside a car
simulator...
take a deep breath and relax into the plush leather seat
behind the wheel...
there is a button marked Start and when you push it, you
hear the motor purr to life
This isn't like any car simulator you have been in before...
You are not trying to win a race...
You are here to remember the joy of driving...
the freedom... the luxury...
the convenience of getting somewhere more quickly than
any other time in history...
You are here to learn patience... to slow down and enjoy
the ride...
Courtesy, grace, and serenity are your goals behind the
wheel of this car...
Take a deep breath... The car smells new...
The gauges are lit in fluorescent blue, green, and red...
The screen shows you are in a parking lot near a

mountain range...
The scenery is breath-taking...
You bask in the 360 degree view the car simulator shows...
The air around you is cool, clean mountain air...
Put the car in drive and you are off...
The GPS (Gods Positioning System) is on, and directs you where to go...
You are told to turn right at the first stop sign...
Although the light ahead of the other cars is red, none of the other drivers will let you in...
Instead of feeling anxious and angry, you notice the button that says...
Pause...
You hit the Pause button to see what happens...
The radio turns on, by itself, and plays a song you love...
You listen and feel the stress leaving...patience is kicking in...
God has programmed this button to aid you any time you feel stressed or anxious...
press Pause and let Him help you...
Someone lets you in...
You wave your thanks and you are on your way...
Breathe in and feel your patience stretching, expanding...
Relax and enjoy the open road... Smile...
You have all you need... nothing can ruin your day or make you anxious...
God is in control...
The road narrows up ahead...
there is a bridge with not much clearance on either side...
You see a Semi, coming the other way...

You are a bit concerned and you think now would be a good time to see what the Angels button does…
You press Angels and you feel some cool air come out of the vents…
It has the scent of incense and lavender…
A sense of calm comes over you and you relax…
You know you will be fine…
The truck driver looks at you and smiles as he passes…
As if he has a secret… Maybe he is one of your angels…
God's angels surround and keep watch over you when you are driving…
Sometimes they are sent to slow you down…
Or to get your attention… Or to keep you alert…
Keep an eye out for your angels today…
You come up behind a car and notice the license plate says Angel One…
There are no coincidences… Have patience and faith in his plan…
Your favorite song comes on the radio and you begin to sing along…
The mountain scenery is gorgeous…
The car rides smoothly around the twists and turns…
You are in your favorite car… on a scenic mountain road…
You don't remember ever being this happy driving…
All drives should be like this…
The feeling of freedom…
The luxury of getting somewhere quickly…
and not having to walk or exert much effort…
Breathe deeply and relax…

Tap Into The Power Of God

You live in a fabulous time with great modern conveniences…
look forward to driving your car today… It is a magic machine!
The richest Roman Emperor never had one!
feel God's patient hand in yours during your drive…
You now know that you can hit the Pause button in your own car at anytime…
The angels surround you but if you feel you need it, you can hit the Angels button…
You know God wants you to remember this feeling, this relaxed easy-going feeling…
His patience goes with you…
Breathe in and relax…
You have reached your destination… A little inn… in the heart of the mountains…
the sign says "Serenity Inn Bed & Breakfast"
As you exit the car to check in, put your new car keys in your pocket…
Take them out during your day, anytime you need patience…
You may need the "Pause" button or the "Angels" button today…
It works inside the car or out!
Feel patience and acceptance surround you as you enter Serenity Inn Bed & Breakfast…
Thank God you are safe and cared for and His serenity is available anytime you need it…

Danielle C. Pace

God's Prescription for Forgiveness

Relax and breathe deeply… Let your mind clear of all thoughts…
Today realize you are not alone…
The Great Spirit of the Universe is here to guide you…
Ask for and receive his help today… God wishes for you to be filled with forgiveness today…
He has given you an unlimited refill of forgiveness…
You may return as often as you like…
See yourself in front of a magnificent building…
This is God's Pharmacy…
Enter in and pause…
You are in a large round Lobby with marble floors and a brightly lit foyer with dark blue seating…
There are 7 more doors arranged around the center of the lobby…
From the left, the doors are Love, Gratitude, Perception, Wisdom, Patience, Forgiveness and Faith
There is a display shelf to your left with many shopping bags of varied colors and patterns to choose from…
Select your favorite bag to put your prescription in…
Breathe deeply and relax…
To fill your prescription for forgiveness, proceed to the door second from the right…
The door has the Mona Lisa painted on it and the word Forgiveness etched in white…
As you open the door, you see a lush, pastoral landscape…
A curvy stone walkway leads up a hill to a small cottage…
The words "The Miracle Studio" hang from a plaque

above the studio door

On your way to the Miracle Studio, you pass a majestic weeping willow tree...

The tree is adorned with brightly colored ribbons tied to its drooping leaves

A small lake lies next to it with 2 beautiful swans floating leisurely...

Feel the tranquility and peace that surrounds you

Walk up the path to the cottage and notice the wrap around porch

There are several rocking chairs and a swing chair

You may come sit and relax here anytime you wish...

Contemplate the beautiful scenery...

Feel the peace and serenity that surrounds you here...

Breathe deeply and enter the artist studio

You find many easels set up around the large room

some have paintings already completed and some are empty

The empty ones are waiting for you to paint...

All of the supplies to paint your forgiveness are here...

Pick a brush and palette and move to one of the empty canvases...

The palette is preloaded with all the colors you will need...

You have the name of someone you need to forgive in mind...

Paint the name of the person on the top left corner of the canvas...

Relax and let the person you need to forgive come to mind...

You begin to paint...

God loves this person and God loves you…
He would like for all of his children to love each other…
Let him tell you why he loves this person…
Remember some of the good times you shared with this person…
The painting begins to take shape…
God tells you this person feels crazy living in this world sometimes the same as you…
It isn't easy for this person to ask for love and maybe they got it totally wrong…
Maybe fear, insecurity, a mental illness or addiction causes this person to strike out at others…
God wants you to pray for this person to know how much God loves them…
As your brush paints this person, you begin to feel their pain…
You feel their uncertainty and you realize, unknowingly they are reaching out for your forgiveness…
The brush moves as if it is infused with the essence of loving forgiveness…
The canvas comes to life as if it feels what you are striving for…
The painting receives God's final touches and is complete!
It is a stirring portrait of all the things that are lovely about this person…
You hear a whirrr and a machine at the center of the studio comes to life
It creates a perfect copy of your painting onto a 5 by 7 printed canvas…
It then adds a custom frame to the print…

Your masterpiece then rolls out into the bin on the right side of the miracle printer...
Pick up the print and put it in your bag...
Add this person to your morning and evening devotion for the next 2 weeks...
Hang the painting somewhere you can see it...
This will help you remember why you are praying for this person...
Every time you forgive someone a miracle happens...
That is why this place is called "The Miracle Studio"...
Miracles happen here... Freedom begins here...
Breathe in and feel God's loving forgiveness envelop you...
On your way out of the studio, there is a table with brightly colored ribbons...
Choose a special ribbon to signify your wish to forgive the person you have painted...
This ribbon is a tie that will connect your hearts back together...
Exit the studio and walk over to your weeping willow tree...
This tree signifies your wish to forgive others...
Each ribbon is a wish for a miracle...
Choose a feathered leave to tie your new ribbon on...
Make a wish that your forgiveness will produce a miracle...
Look at all the ribbons you have tied to your tree...
Each one has connected your heart to another...
Each one has melted the time that you need to spend in morbid reflection...

Rejoice and be glad for all your miracles...
Each tied ribbon affirms you are returning to who you
truly are, a person full of God's loving forgiveness...
The exit back to the lobby appears before you...
As you close the door, remember to view your masterpiece
throughout the day...
Breathe deeply...
Thank God for his forgiveness... Extend this forgiveness
to others...
Enjoy the freedom that comes from forgiving others and
pray that your forgiveness creates miracles in the world
today...

God's Prescription for Faith

Relax and breathe deeply... Let your mind clear of all
thoughts...
Today realize you are not alone...
The Great Spirit of the Universe is here to show you...
Ask for and receive faith today... God wishes for you to be
full of faith today...
He has given you an unlimited refill of faith...
You may return as often as you like...
See yourself in front of a magnificent building...
This is God's Pharmacy...
Enter in and pause... Breathe deeply...
You are in a large Lobby with marble floors and a
brightly lit foyer with dark blue seating...
There are 7 more doors arranged around the center of the
lobby...

*From the left, the doors are Love, Gratitude, Perception,
Wisdom, Patience, Forgiveness and Faith
Breathe deeply and relax...
To fill your prescription for faith, Proceed to the door on
your far right...
the door is painted sky blue with white fluffy clouds and
has the word Faith written in white upon it...
There is no handle but your faith has opened the door on
your approach...
as the door opens, you see a large archway floating near
you with a sign saying "Angel University"
Enter in and look around...
You seem to be standing among the clouds... more like
floating...
You feel something weird on your back...
You have a pair of wings on your back!!
Look around... there are many students, floating or flying
about...
They also have wings... some are small, some are very
large...
The door attendant asks if you have your book bag...
If you don't, he hands you a book bag and tells you your
very special Angel textbook is in it...
Also your Faith journal and a feather quill pen...
He says "Keep them with you and bring them back
whenever you come to the University..."
Your first class is an open circle of desks arranged around
a podium...
Float over to the desks, choose one and sit down...
relax and take a deep breath...*

As the other students take their seats a trumpet sounds…
Then a beautiful angel floats in playing a violin…
The sound is mesmerizing… She takes her place at the
podium
She announces herself as Professor Laureate and
ArchAngel Gabriel
She says this class is an intense study of Faith
"This class is meant to help you build your spiritual
muscles
and grow your wings so that you can graduate to Flight
School"
She says each day is a day when your faith will be tested…
She tells you to relax when taking these tests, they will
pass and you will be fine
"Let faith guide you"…
She instructs you to read the current chapter in your
Angel textbook during the day
This will help you with the tests and help you gain faith
You will find steps you can take to master the challenges
that are presented…
Relax and be happy to be in this very special class…
You can feel the spiritual light beams vibrating in this
place…
a bright radiant light reaches out from the center where
Arch Angel Gabriel is
The Professor tells you to take out your journal
She instructs "Anytime you feel you are being tested
today write down what is happening
How can you reach out in faith in this situation?
How can you contact God to enlist his help?

Tap Into The Power Of God

Read in your textbook, then write in your journal
Write out your feelings regarding the test and how you
can trust and rely on God
This is how you will grow in faith…"
She opens her wings and slowly and elegantly flaps them
and rises above the class
As she is flying overhead she says
"This is how you begin turning your will over and letting
Him guide you…
this is how you will grow your glorious wings…"
It is exciting to see the beautiful Arch Angel Gabriel
flying so gracefully…
She lands next to your desk and says
"Take a deep breath and listen to the humming of
spiritual energy all about you…
This is the flow you are joining in faith…
This sixth sense connects you to your brothers and sisters
and to God…"
She flies back to the podium
She says if you have finished a step in your text,
have your journal out and ready for her to review
As you pass each step, the next one will appear in your
textbook…
Your wings will grow a foot longer with each step you
complete
There are 12 steps in the text and when you finish, you
will graduate to flight school!
If you have completed a step, stay after to review your
work with Gabriel
Pause the meditation and meditate quietly for 2 or 3

minutes if you have work to review
*If you have no work to review, or once you are through
with your review,*
*float over to the University Cafe and join your fellow
students for refreshments*
*The Cafe is a large glass dome with trays of food laid out
in buffet style in the center*
Get a plate of refreshments and sit with your friends
*Everyone is excited to be at the University and hoping to
get to Flight School soon*
talk focuses on what everyone is learning about faith
*You can see the flight school students learning to fly
outside the Cafeteria glass...*
You can't wait to join them...
*After finishing, drop off your tray and head outside
Breathe deeply...*
The exit back to the lobby appears before you...
*As you close the door to Angel University, remember to
read your textbook chapter and write in your journal
today...*
*Thank God for appointing the lovely ArchAngel Gabriel
to help you grow in Faith...*

Disclaimer

The excerpts from *Alcoholics Anonymous,* the Big Book and *Twelve Steps and Twelve Traditions* are reprinted with permission of Alcoholics Anonymous World Services, Inc. ("A.A.W.S."). Permission to reprint these excerpts does not mean that A.A.W.S. has reviewed or approved the contents of this publication, or that A.A. necessarily agrees with the views expressed herein. A.A. is a program of recovery from alcoholism only – use of this excerpt in connection with programs and activities which are patterned after A.A., but which address other problems, or in any other non-A.A. context, does not imply otherwise.

About the Author

Danielle C. Pace

Danielle has been writing most of her life but mostly in code, as she is a software developer by trade. She recently started feeling the urge to put pen to paper and explore the world of words which has always fascinated her. She began with writing and publishing a book of poetry "Twisted Lines" in 2018 after feeling some divine inspiration. This latest book came about after an early morning wakeup call by her manager requesting a book on her adventure with the 12 steps of AA, and a generic version of the 12 steps that could help anyone who is embarking on a journey of spiritual growth.

Danielle feels she was led to the halls of Alcoholics Anonymous when a bout of depression had taken over and self-medicating with alcohol led her to feel even more hopeless. In desperation she turned to AA. In AA she found a solution in the 12 steps, which helped her to place herself under God's care. Having had a spiritual awakening, as a result of doing the 12 steps, she then let God take over as the manager of her life.

Danielle's spiritual journey isn't over, but she wants to share the steps she took in the beginning for anyone who is unsure where to start. Here's hoping that your journey will lead you to a world that is happy, joyous and free!

Danielle grew up in Orange Park, Florida, lived for some years on the Big Island of Hawaii and in St. Petersburg, Florida and now resides in Naples, Florida.

Printed in the United States
by Baker & Taylor Publisher Services